Art Projects by Design

Art Projects by Design

A Guide for the Classroom

Del Klaustermeier

1997
TEACHER IDEAS PRESS
Libraries Unlimited
A Division of Greenwood Publishing Group, Inc.
Englewood, Colorado

Dedicated to the sources of my greatest pride,
Anne and Leigh

TEACHER IDEAS PRESS
Libraries Unlimited
A Division of Greenwood Publishing Group, Inc.
P.O. Box 6633
Englewood, CO 80155-6633
1-800-237-6124
www.lu.com/tip

Production Editor: Kevin W. Perizzolo
Editorial Assistant: Shannon Graff
Copy Editor: Jason Cook
Proofreader: Eileen Bartlett
Interior Design and Layout: Judy Gay Matthews

Library of Congress Cataloging-in-Publication Data

Klaustermeier, Del, 1950-
    Art projects by design : a guide for the classroom / by Del
Klaustermeier.
        xi, 207 p. 22x28 cm.
        Includes bibliographical references and index.
        ISBN 1-56308-441-4
        1. Art--Study and teaching (Elementary)--United States.
    2. Learning by discovery. 3. Activity programs in education--United
States. I. Title.
    N362.K63   1997
    372.5'044'0973--dc21   96-30085
                                                            CIP

Contents

Preface

"Del, why don't you write up the directions for your art projects? I'd love to do some of them in my classroom."

After hearing this statement numerous times over a period of 10 years from classroom teachers as well as art teachers, I decided to write this book. My goal was to provide the teacher with a brief, but concise, overview of the design elements and step-by-step directions for art projects with art history references. I wanted to include art projects that could be easily integrated in as many curricular areas as possible. Additionally, I wanted student-made examples to serve as visual references.

I firmly believe that art education is an integral and beneficial component of every child's education. With this book and a joint effort between teachers and students, the educational benefits and personal growth can be limitless for all involved.

Acknowledgments

Many thanks go to:

- Ralph Osterberg and Jenny Faherty, for their excellent photography skills.
- Rebecca White and Connie Hayes, who helped me become computer literate.
- Barbara, Dick, Karen, Bill, Greg, Sherrie, and Barbara, for moral support.
- Maryd, Cookie, and Terri, for their expert assistance.
- All art teacher friends and art students who shared ideas with me so I could adapt them for this book.

Every effort has been made to contact the students whose work appears in this book. I regret any oversights that may have occurred and would be happy to rectify them with a printed correction.

Introduction

Teaching art at the elementary level provides both the student and the teacher with the opportunity not only to develop their artistic skills but also to enhance their awareness of the world and its varied cultures. Art additionally provides the chance to gain an appreciation of the various styles of art and artists. An art program that incorporates a wide variety of materials and techniques offers endless possibilities for artistic endeavors. Most important, art education allows the students to grow as individuals whose creations are unique, valuable, and a means of learning more than just art concepts.

The ideas found in this book are based on eight design elements: composition, line, area, texture, value, color, space, and three-dimensional art. Each chapter begins with a brief overview of the design element with suggested art history references. Each art project lists the necessary materials, directions for the teacher, design elements that are incorporated, art history references, and a suggested grade level. Each section of activities begins with lower-primary ideas, proceeds to intermediate-level ideas, and ends with upper-elementary ideas.

Feel free to adapt the project ideas to fit your classroom and the materials you have available. Many of the projects offer excellent opportunities for integration with social studies, math, science, and language arts lessons. You and your students will create unique pieces of art, but more important, the excitement of learning about art and creating art will become a valuable part of the educational process taking place in your classroom.

For Further Reading

Dorra, Henri. *Art in Perspective.* New York: Harcourt, Brace, Jovanovich, 1973.

Feldman, Edmund Burke. *Varieties of Visual Experience--Image and Idea.* Englewood Cliffs, New Jersey: Prentice-Hall and New York: Henry N. Abrams, n.d.

Janson, Anthony F. *History of Art.* Englewood Cliffs, New Jersey: Prentice-Hall and New York: Henry N. Abrams, 1991.

Lauer, David. *Design Basics.* New York: Rinehart and Winston, 1979.

Lucie-Smith, Edward. *Art Now.* New York: William Morrow, 1977.

Ocvirk, Otto, et al. *Art Fundamentals: Theory and Practice.* 7th ed. Madison, Wisconsin: Brown and Benchmark, 1994.

Preble, Duane, and Diane Preble. *Artforms.* New York: HarperCollins, 1989.

Richardson, John Adkins. *Art--The Way It Is.* New York: Henry Abrams, 1980.

Rogers, Rosalind. *Art Talk.* Mission Hills, California: Glencoe, 1988.

Shorewood Collection Art Reference Guide. New York: Shorewood Fine Art, 1985.

Chapter

1

Composition

Types of Compositions

The foundation for any art project uses the design element of **composition**, also called **form**. Through the study of composition, students consider how they wish to place objects on paper, the **picture plane**. The choices consist of four basic composition types: **symmetrical**, **asymmetrical**, **repetition**, and **radial**. Any art project or piece of fine art will use one of these formats.

Symmetrical Composition

In a **symmetrical composition**, an object and its mirror image appear on opposite sides of an imagined center line on the paper. An example from nature would be a butterfly's wing design. The student imagines a vertical center line on the paper. After placing an object on one side of the paper, the student must place a mirror image of the same object on the other side of the center line. A horizontal center line with mirror images can also be a variation of symmetry. Art work by Erté and building decoration from the Art Nouveau style use a symmetrical compositional format.

For the advanced student, a discussion of **approximate symmetry** becomes appropriate. In this compositional format, the student symmetrically places objects of similar shape, not exact mirror images. For example, Grant Wood's *American Gothic* displays an approximate symmetrical arrangement with the placement of his figures in relation to the home in the background. Leonardo Da Vinci's *Last Supper* also incorporates an approximate symmetrical composition.

Asymmetrical Composition

An **asymmetrical composition**, the most commonly used format, involves the random placement of objects on a picture plane that is to be used in its entirety. This compositional type requires the development of **felt composition**; that is, after a student places an object on one side of the paper, he or she must "feel" what object or objects to place on the other side of the paper to achieve a balanced composition. The student must turn the paper around looking at it upside down and from all views to see if each side of the composition either contains too many objects or appears empty when compared to the other side. The student will develop a "feeling" for the overall balance of the picture plane. Edgar Degas's *Dancers Practicing at the Barre* is an excellent example of an asymmetrical composition.

Repetition Composition

A **repetition composition** contains some type of repeating pattern, or **motif**, whether very simple or very complex. For example, a folded paper-doll cut-out contains a repetition of the same doll. More elaborate repetition compositions may contain a combination of color, line, and shape patterns repeating in an intricate pattern. An easily accessible source for examples is a wallpaper book. Numerous art history examples may be found in Greek and Native American pottery. Andy Warhol's *Campbell Soup Cans* shows a simple repetition composition of soup cans (but with no repetition in the order of the kinds of soup cans). Edward Hopper's *Early Sunday Morning* contains an intricate repeating composition.

ψρ

Radial Composition

A ***radial composition*** repeats in a circular fashion; that is, the composition has a center point around which the design repeats. The circular "frame" is sectioned equally into pieces (like a pie), and the same design repeats in each of the sections. The design may be drawn the same way in each section or reversed in every other section. A kaleidoscope makes use of radial composition. Radial compositions are found in spider webs, hubcap designs, Chartes Cathedral's Gothic rose windows, Pennsylvania Dutch hex designs, and Maurice Utrillo's *Sacré Coeur, Monmartre et Rue Saint Rustique*.

Subject Matter

Once the student has decided upon one of the four compositional types, he or she must consider how to represent the ***subject matter***, the object or objects to be portrayed. The subject matter may be drawn in an ***objective***, ***subjective***, or ***non-objective approach***. For the sake of discussion, a leaf will be used to illustrate the difference between the three manners of representation.

Objective Approach

With the ***objective approach***, the composition contains a realistic depiction of the subject matter. Through careful observation, the student draws the shapes, lines, textures, and colors of the leaf. The work of William Harnett, especially *After the Hunt*, offers examples of subject matter presented in a realistic, objective approach.

Subjective Approach

With the ***subjective approach***, the composition contains a personal interpretation of the subject matter. For example, the student may choose to draw the basic shape of the leaf without realistic details. The leaf may also be abstracted, but the shape is still recognizable as a leaf. In Pablo Picasso's *Les Demoiselles d'Avignon*, the viewer can recognize the figures as females, but they are distorted and abstracted.

Non-Objective Approach

With the ***non-objective approach***, the composition contains no recognizable depiction of the subject matter. In this case, the leaf is used as a springboard for study of the design elements. For example, the student may base the composition on the movement of a leaf in various settings. The student would decide what types of lines show the movement of a leaf in a windstorm, in a gently flowing river, or in a tornado. Jackson Pollock's action painting *Autumn Rhythm* is an example of the non-objective approach—through Pollock's use of lines of colors, the painting records the artist's movement rather than realistic or abstracted objects.

Principles of Organization

After the student has decided upon compositional type and the manner in which to draw the subject matter, he or she must apply the ***principles of organization***. Simply defined, principles of organization deal with the concerns of design and balance that the student manipulates to make the composition visually appealing. The principles of organization include ***harmony, variety, balance, movement, rhythm, proportion, dominance, and economy***.

Harmony

Harmony indicates that the objects in the composition work together. Using a leaf design again as an example, the student may choose to use one type of leaf in the composition. However, if the student decides to include a bird, this would destroy the harmony within the composition. With the introduction of a bird in a composition of leaves, the bird becomes dominant because its shape and colors differ from the leaves. Jasper Johns's harmonic *Gray Numbers* incorporates a variety of numbers that appear to repeat, but each one is subtly varied.

Variety

The student must consider *variety*; that is, what contrast or variation will make the composition interesting and unique. With this consideration, the student may decide to show a variety of leaves in the composition instead of just one type. In Stuart Davis's *Swing Landscaper*, an assortment of geometric shapes are arranged to create interest and variety. Davis offers the viewer a variety of shapes to observe in a harmonic composition that contains repeating and similar colors and shapes.

Balance

Balance is the placement of the subject matter in the picture plane in a visually pleasing manner. When balance is achieved, every part of the picture plane becomes an integral part of the composition. No part will appear too busy or too empty. The viewer finds something interesting to see throughout the entire composition. The arrangement of lines and colors in Piet Mondrian's *Composition in White, Black, and Red* is an example of balance throughout the picture plane.

Movement

Movement refers to how the viewer's eye moves around the composition; that is, how the objects take the viewer's eye from one part of the picture plane to another. This movement will have some type of **rhythm** (see below). The lines and shapes in John Marin's *Phippsburg, Maine* help the viewer's eye move from one part of the composition to the other.

Rhythm

The **rhythm** of a composition refers to how the viewer's eye moves in a circular, vertical, horizontal, or even in a "letter of the alphabet" rhythm movement throughout the composition. For example, a triangular rhythm can be thought of as the letter *A* whereas a circular rhythm can be the letter *O*. The horizontal lines and repeating windows and doors in Edward Hopper's *Early Sunday Morning* offer a calm yet repeating rhythm.

Proportion

The student must consider the **proportion** of the objects within the composition. For example, has the student drawn the stem of a leaf in proportion to the body of the leaf? Has the student drawn different types of leaves in proportion to each other? Is a maple leaf smaller or larger than an aspen leaf? The student also needs to decide if the remaining **negative shapes**, the background shapes, are too large or too small when compared to the space that the **positive shapes**, the actual objects, occupy in the picture plane. Often the student will not draw objects large enough, leaving negative areas that make the picture plane appear empty. *Nuit de Noel* by Henri Matisse is a pleasing balance of positive and negative shapes. The proportion of the shapes, whether positive or negative, complement each other and all shapes are equally important for a balanced composition.

The Matisse piece represents a non-distorted proportion. The Surrealist René Magritte deliberately used distortion of proportion to portray a fantasy scene in *The Listening Chamber*, causing the viewer to ask, Is the apple of normal size inside a small room or is it a huge apple inside a normal-size room?

Dominance

To understand the concept of **dominance**, the student must decide what object to use as the **focal point**. In other words, what object appears to be the center of interest and how do the other objects revolve around this center to bring the viewer's eye back? Ways of creating a focal point include making the chosen object a different size or color than the other objects or placing it somewhere near the center of the picture plane. Georges Seurat's *A Sunday Afternoon on the Island of La Grande Jatte* affords the viewer an interesting composition in which a little girl in white remains the focal point in a landscape filled with many larger objects and people.

Economy

The principle of **economy** requires the decision-making ability of knowing when to stop. The student must know when a part of the composition appears too "busy" when compared with another part. The student would then simplify the design by eliminating some lines, shapes, or colors rather than add more to make the other part of the design just as "busy." Paul Cezanne's still-life and landscape paintings are filled with shapes of color, but not to the point of overwhelming the viewer's eye. Frank Stella's *Sinjerli Variation I* has very few shapes and colors but retains an interesting composition.

Unity

If the student has created his or her composition using the principles of design, it should have **unity**; that is, every component contributes to a visually pleasing piece of art. Michelangelo's Sistine Chapel ceiling, with its vast scale, hundreds of figures, and architectural components, maintains a feeling of unity. Every aspect of this amazing creation has a purpose and importance within the overall composition.

Media

The student must decide which **media** to use. The student's fine motor development, or the lack of it, dictates what media will be appropriate. For example, a first-grade student can manipulate felt-tip markers more successfully than color pencil to color in shapes. Likewise, a sixth-grade student has the fine motor development to work with linoleum carving tools, brayers, and printer's ink. Whether using crayons, tempera paint, clay, or printer's ink, the student must also be aware of the variety of **techniques** available with each medium.

Technique

Technique refers to how the student uses or applies the medium or media. For example, crayons may be used for simply coloring a white piece of paper or crayons and tempera paint together may be used to achieve a crayon-resist technique. A comparison of Hans Holbein's *Henry VIII*, an example of glaze-painting technique, and Vincent Van Gogh's *Starry Night*, an example of the encaustic technique, shows how the technique used with oil paint can be vastly different.

Purpose or Meaning

A final consideration for the student pertains to the question, What is the *purpose* or *meaning* of my art? Depending upon the grade level of the student, the composition's purpose may be to study an *art concept*, to explore the *plastic quality* of a media, or to relay a *message*.

Art Concept

At the elementary level, the purpose may be to study a specific *art concept*, such as a design element or a principle of organization. At this level, the project's purpose may be simply to learn how to create a simple symmetrical design with construction paper.

Plastic Quality

The purpose may be to explore the *plastic quality* of a given design element or media. For example, the student might create different symmetrical arrangements using geometric shapes of construction paper or create different hues of blue using blue and white tempera paint. The work of Piet Mondrian offers an excellent springboard for studying composition through his balance of color shapes and black lines. Claude Monet's paintings can be used to analyze various color theories such as monochromatic, analogous, and complementary color relationships.

Message

For the advanced student, the project's purpose might be to relay a *message*. The composition becomes a visual representation of the student's feelings and thoughts, speaking to the viewer. Pablo Picasso's *Guernica* is an excellent example of art that relays a message—in this case, the horrors of war.

Art History

The inclusion of the study of *art history*, the chronicle of artistic periods and styles, exposes the student to the wonderfully varied ways and means that artists have represented their worlds and their perceptions of their lives. When an art project is referenced to an artist or a period of art, it offers more than the chance to learn an art concept. The project affords a means of associating and understanding the importance of art in the history of humanity and the opportunity to be a creative participant. The student will realize that, for many civilizations, art and architecture provide an important cultural record. Much has been learned about the Egyptian, Assyrian, and Babylonian civilizations through the surviving art and architecture. The art and architecture of African tribes and the Mayan and Aztec cultures record their lives and beliefs. Art has been and will continue to be a tool for humanity to record and make known thoughts and beliefs about life.

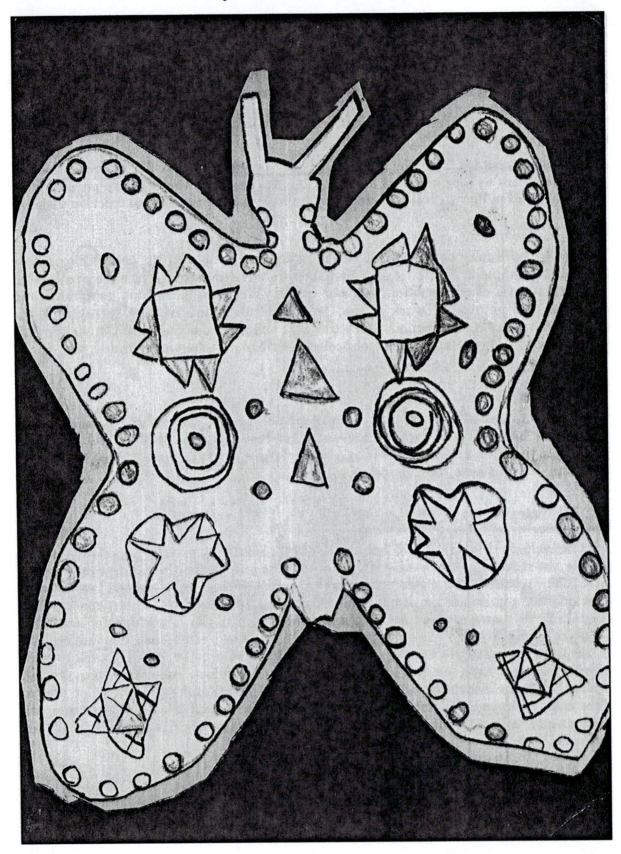

Materials

- oil pastels
- 2 sheets 9-by-12-inch white construction paper
- 1 sheet 9-by-12-inch construction paper, any color
- scissors
- tape
- pencil
- glue

Directions

Have students:

1. On a sheet of 9-by-12-inch white construction paper, draw a wiggle line that touches all four edges.

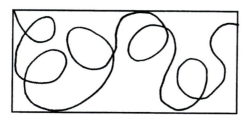

2. Color all shapes with oil pastels.

3. On the second sheet of 9-by-12-inch white construction paper, draw a symmetrical silhouette butterfly shape lengthwise.

4. Fold the butterfly paper in half lengthwise with the butterfly on the outside vertically.

5. With the butterfly paper still folded, draw various lines and shapes on one side to decorate the wings.

6. At a window, light source (i.e., light table), or with carbon paper, transfer the lines and shapes onto the other side of the paper, so that the lines and shapes become symmetrical.

7. Open the butterfly paper and tape the construction paper with the butterfly on top of the colored construction paper with oil pastel.

8. With a pencil, retrace the lines and fill in the shapes on the butterfly. Wherever pressure is applied, the oil pastel will transfer to the back of the butterfly paper, creating a simple monoprint.

9. Remove the construction paper with oil pastel.

10. Cut out the butterfly and glue onto any color of 9-by-12-inch construction paper.

Option for a Border Effect: Cut ½ inch beyond the contour edge of the butterfly and glue onto another piece of 9-by-12-inch construction paper that is a different color.

Design Element: Composition—symmetrical and decorative use of line and shapes

Art History: Pablo Picasso for decorative lines and shapes; Erté for symmetrical composition

Grade Level: Lower primary

Materials

- practice paper with five pre-drawn tie shapes on it
- Six to eight tie-shaped tagboard templates
- scraps of construction paper cut to various widths; colors should encompass the color wheel
- 1-by-12-inch black construction paper for tie bar from which ties appear to hang
- 12-by-18-inch tagboard, any color
- hole punch
- glue
- scissors
- felt-tip markers

Directions

Have students:

1. With felt-tip markers, using practice paper, plan out five tie patterns using at least three of your analogous colors.

2. From the five practice ties, select the three best patterns.

3. Select construction paper to match the analogous colors of the selected patterns.

4. At a window, light source (i.e., light table), or with carbon paper, transfer the tie template onto the three analogous colors of construction paper. For each of the three ties, glue scraps of the two remaining colors to create the patterns selected in step 2. Glue down scraps of construction paper so they extend beyond the edge of the tie, then cut along the original tie pattern for a final, clean edge.

5. Glue 1-by-12-inch black construction paper on tagboard for a tie bar. Glue ties so they appear to hang from the tie bar.

Design Element: Composition—repetition; Color—analogous colors

Art History: Andy Warhol for repetition; Victor Vasarely for color

Grade Level: Lower primary

Materials

- 12-by-18-inch tagboard
- pencil
- oil pastels (white, gray, light blue, blue, violet, and pink)
- black tempera paint, slightly diluted

- scissors
- paintbrush
- 12-by-18-inch construction paper in "winter colors," that is, white, gray, light blue, violet, and pink.

Directions

Have students:

1. On 12-by-18-inch tagboard, use a pencil to draw a large *X* with a vertical line through the center.

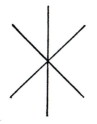

Using one *O*, one *V*, and one short straight line, draw a design on one arm of the snowflake. Repeat the design on the five remaining arms.

3. Choose three colors of oil pastel from the following list of "winter colors": white, gray, light blue, blue, violet, pink.

4. At a window, light source (i.e., light table), or with carbon paper, transfer all lines with one color of oil pastel.

5. Outline the snowflake with a second color.

6. Outline the snowflake a second time with the third color.

7. Brush the snowflake with only one coat of slightly diluted black tempera. The black tempera will not adhere to the oil pastel, allowing the snowflake pattern to appear on a black background. If brushed twice, the black tempera will adhere to the oil pastel, obscuring the snowflake design.

8. Cut out the snowflake and mount it on any "winter color" of construction paper.

Design Element: Composition—radial

Art History: Gothic rose window for radial composition

Grade Level: Lower elementary

Materials

- 12-by-18-inch construction paper, any color
- 2 sheets 4-by-12-inch construction paper, different color than the 12-by-18-inch construction paper.
- glue
- scissors
- pencil

Directions

Have students:

1. Choose any color of 12-by-18-inch construction paper and one or two colors of 4-by-12-inch construction paper.

2. Draw as many shapes as desired on each of the 12-inch edges of the 4-by-12-inch sheets. Choose from the following choices of shapes:

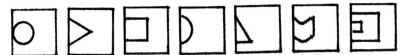

Shapes inside of shapes are an option:

4. Cut out the shapes and set aside.

5. Glue down the remainder of the cut 4-by-12-inch sheet on 12-by-18-inch construction paper. The 12-inch length of the 4-by-12 sheet should be glued on the 12-inch length of the 12-by-18 construction paper.

6. Place the cut-out pieces back into the original shapes (without glue).

7. Put glue on them, flip them over, and glue them in a symmetrical fashion with respect to the cut edge of the 4-by-12-inch sheet. For shapes within shapes, glue the inside shape in its original position.

Design Element: Composition—symmetry; Area—positive and negative shapes

Art History: Henri Matisse for cut-paper designs

Grade Level: Lower primary

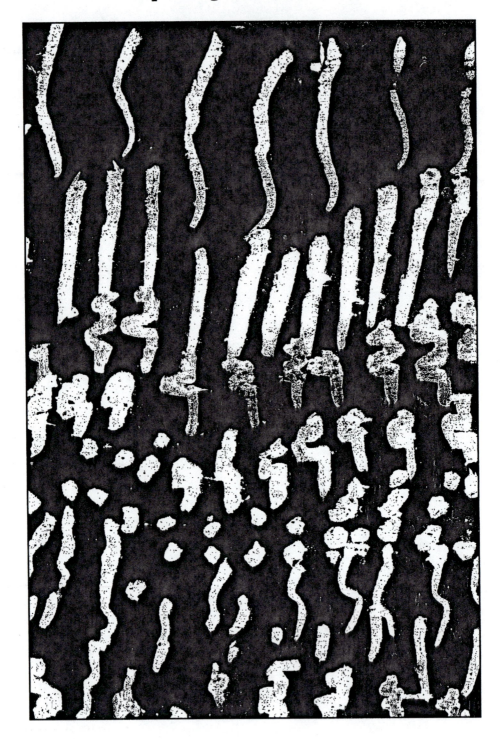

Materials

- 12-by-18-inch tagboard
- 6-by-18-inch tagboard
- oil pastels

- black tempera paint, slightly diluted
- paintbrush
- scissors

Directions

Have students:

1. Draw mountain line lengthwise on 6-by-18-inch tagboard.

2. Cut out the mountain line, keeping the bottom piece as a template.

3. On 12-by-18-inch tagboard placed vertically, set the left edge of the mountain line template at the upper left edge of the tagboard. (Six inches of the template will extend past the right edge of the tagboard.) Using any color of oil pastel, draw vertical lines from the edge of the template to the top of the tagboard.

4. Move mountain template down one inch and to the left one inch and draw vertical lines from the mountain edge with another color of oil pastel. The short, straight lines should begin at the edge of the template and end at the bottom of the line directly above (i.e., fill the space between the template and the previous line).

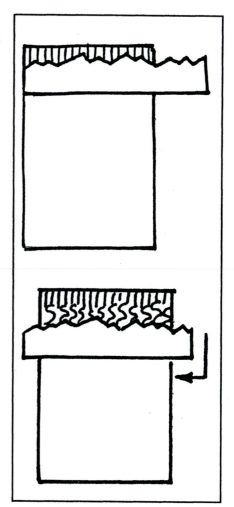

5. Repeat step 4 until the entire tagboard is filled. When the right edge of the template reaches the right edge of the tagboard, move down one inch and to the right one inch.

6. Apply one coat of slightly diluted black tempera paint. The tempera should not adhere to the oil pastel.

Variation: Choose five colors of oil pastel. For each color, choose a specific line design. Use in repeating order.

Design Element: Composition—repetition; Line—line variety

Art History: Warhol for repetition

Grade Level: Lower primary

Materials

- two 3-by-3-inch Styrofoam sheets (from trays commonly used for meat packaging)
- 9-by-12-inch construction paper
- 3-inch-wide strip of tagboard
- tempera paint, different colors
- paintbrush
- pencil
- scissors

Directions

Have students:

1. Draw two different flowers, one on each of the 3-by-3-inch Styrofoam sheets. Make the flowers touch an edge or edges of the Styrofoam.

2. Cut out the flowers.

3. Choose three analogous colors, two for the paint and one for the paper.

4. Using a 3-inch-wide strip of tagboard, draw a grid system (slightly wider than the flower) on a sheet of construction paper.

5. Brush paint onto one of the Styrofoam flowers and print one flower in every other square. The rows should alternate like a checkerboard.

6. Brush paint onto the second Styrofoam flower and print one flower in each remaining square.

Design Element: Composition—repetition; Color—analogous colors

Art History: Warhol for repetition

Grade Level: Lower primary

Materials

- three 3-inch squares tagboard
- 12-inch-diameter circle template
- 12-by-18-inch white tagboard
- oil pastels
- black tempera paint, slightly diluted
- paintbrush
- glue
- scissors
- pencil

Directions

Have students:

1. Draw three different flowers, one on each of the three squares of tagboard, creating three flower templates.

2. At a window, light source (i.e., light table), or with carbon paper, transfer the circle template onto white tagboard.

3. Cut out the flowers and the circle.

4. Start by tracing one of the three flower templates in the center of the circle on the white tagboard. Using one of the remaining flower templates, trace a ring of flowers around the first flower. With the remaining flower template, trace a ring of flowers around the previous ring of flowers.

5. Color in the flowers with oil pastels. Use at least two colors for each flower type.

6. Color the background spaces, leaving a ¼-inch space between the flower and the background color.

7. Apply one coat of slightly diluted black tempera paint to the circle and the flowers. To get a good "resist," dip the paintbrush in water first, then in paint, and apply only one coat—do not brush over a second time.

Option: Cut out the "bouquet" and glue onto a doily. Glue the doily onto construction paper.

Design Element: Composition—radial

Art History: Gothic rose window for radial composition

Grade Level: Lower primary

Materials

- 12-by-18-inch construction paper, any color
- 9-by-12-inch construction paper, the same color as the 12-by-18-inch sheet
- glue

- 2 sheets of 9-by-12-inch construction paper the same color, any color but the color used previously
- scissors
- stapler

Directions

Have students:

1. On a sheet of 12-by-18-inch construction paper, glue one sheet of 9-by-12-inch construction paper of another color. The 12-inch edges should line up to divide the 12-by-18-inch paper in half.

2. Staple the two remaining sheets of 9-by-12-inch paper together.

3. Cut out different geometric shapes from the two stapled sheets of paper, making two different colors of each shape.

4. Glue cut-out geometric shapes of one color onto the half of the 12-by-18-inch paper that is the second color. For example, if the colors are red and green, glue the green shape on the red side and the red shape on the green side. Glue the shapes symmetrically with respect to the center line on the 12-by-18-inch paper.

5. Continue to glue shapes symmetrically until a balanced symmetrical design is created in the picture plane. Shapes may be glued inside of shapes but be sure to alternate colors.

Design Element: Composition—symmetry with shapes; positive and negative shapes

Art History: Grant Wood, Frank Stella for symmetry

Grade Level: Lower primary and up

Materials

- 12-by-18-inch white construction paper, tagboard, or watercolor paper
- watercolor paint
- paintbrush
- black felt-tip pen

Directions

Have students:

1. Paint three flowers anywhere on the paper or tagboard: start with dabs of yellow in the middle, then orange, then red. Make two rows of dabs for each color (be sure to dab, not *stab* with the paintbrush).

2. Paint three additional flowers anywhere on the paper or tagboard: start with dabs of red in the middle, then orange, then yellow.

3. Paint leaves using green and yellow-green dabs. Each flower should have three leaves. Make two rows of dabs for each color of green.

4. Paint the background using blue and violet dabs.

5. With a black felt-tip pen, outline each row of dabs. Each flower should have six of these lines, and each leaf four.

Design Element: Composition—asymmetrical composition
Art History: Georges Seurat for Pointillism and asymmetrical composition
Grade Level: Lower primary

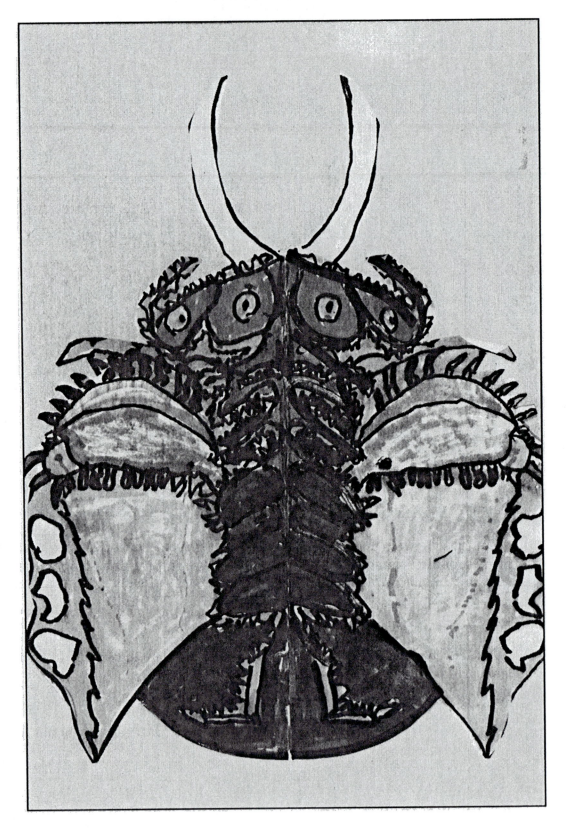

Materials

- 12-by-18-inch white construction paper
- 12-by-18-inch construction paper, any color
- black marker (permanent)
- felt-tip markers
- scissors
- glue
- pencil

Directions

Have students:

1. Fold a sheet of 12-by-18-inch construction paper in half lengthwise. Unfold the paper. The teacher or student writes the student's name along the fold, using the fold as the baseline (cursive is suggested). Letters that extend below the baseline (e.g., *f, g, p, y, j*) are acceptable, including capitals (e.g., *2, 9, 3*).

2. At a window, light source (i.e., light table), or with carbon paper, transfer the name through the paper to the other side of the baseline with a pencil (letters that extend below the baseline will need to be traced back to the original half of the paper).

3. Trace the names with black marker.

4. Using the name shape as a body, make a symmetrical name creature, deciding where to add eyes, hands, feet, and so on. Draw each feature on one side of the baseline and trace onto the other side so that features are symmetrical. Be sure to use the whole paper. Those with short names will need to add legs, fins, tails, as well as some type of head appendages: horns, large ears, spiked hair, and so on.

5. With felt-tip markers, color the shapes in the name creature.

6. Cut out the name creature and glue onto construction paper.

Design Element: Composition—symmetry
Art History: Grant Wood's *American Gothic* for symmetry
Grade Level: Lower primary

Turtle Shell Patterns

Materials

- 12-by-18-inch tagboard
- oil pastels
- black tempera paint, slightly diluted
- paintbrush
- construction paper

- stapler
- scissors
- oval template (turtle shell)
- visual references of various turtle heads, legs, and tails

Directions

Have students:

1. At a window, light source (i.e., light table), or with carbon paper, transfer the turtle shell template onto 12-by-18-inch tagboard.

2. Draw another oval inside that follows the contour of the shell.

3. Draw four or five horizontal parallel lines inside the shell.

4. Draw *V*'s connecting the parallel lines at both ends.

5. Draw horizontal lines from the points of the *V*'s to the oval and angled lines from the ends of upper and lower parallel lines.

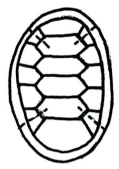

6. Draw concentric shapes inside each shape using three colors of oil pastel.

7. Paint with one coat of slightly diluted black tempera paint. (The paint should not adhere to the oil pastel.)

8. Draw a head and four legs on any color of construction paper.

9. Cut out the head and legs. Cut out the shell and make four cuts along the dotted lines shown in the figure above.

10. Overlap the two cut edges at each slit and staple together so that the shell "pops up."

11. Staple on the head and legs at the edge of the shell.

12. Staple the completed turtle onto any color of construction paper. Staple at the edge of the shell. The head and appendages should lie flat on the construction paper.

Design Element: Composition—radial; Line—concentric

Art History: Radial composition found in nature

Grade Level: Intermediate

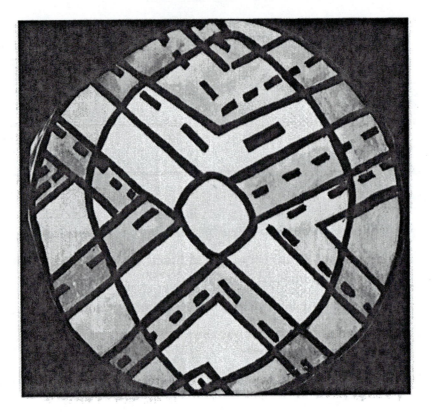

Materials

- practice paper with four 3-inch diameter circles
- copier paper pie shapes; one each of 1/3, 1/4, 1/5, 1/6, and 1/8 of a 6-inch-radius circle
- five 12-inch-diameter circle templates; one each of 1/3, 1/4, 1/5, 1/6, and 1/8 divisions marked and with a pencil-point hole at the center
- 12-by-18-inch black construction paper
- 12-by-18-inch white construction paper
- watercolor paint
- black marker
- carbon paper or student-created carbon paper
- scissors
- pencil

Directions

Have students:

1. Create four practice hubcap designs. Choose the best design.

2. Determine whether the hubcap design repeats 3, 4, 5, 6, or 8 times within a circle to determine which pie shape to use. Draw the design on the pie shape. If the hubcap design repeats three times, draw 1/3 of the hubcap design in the 1/3 pie shape.

3. At a window, light source (i.e., light table), or with carbon paper, transfer circle template onto 12-by-18-inch construction paper. Be sure to mark the center hole of the template. Trace the pie shape design by placing the point of the pie shape on the center dot. Repeat until the circle is filled.

4. For an even number of pie shapes, the design should be reversed—traced upside down—in every other pie shape.

5. Outline the design with black marker.

6. Color with watercolor paint in a repeating pattern.

7. Cut out the design and mount on 12-by-18-inch black construction paper.

Design Element: Composition—radial

Art History: Gothic rose window; Pennsylvania Dutch hex designs for radial composition

Grade Level: Intermediate

Materials

- 3-by-3-inch paper
- 3-by-3-inch Styrofoam square (meat trays work well)
- pencil
- scissors
- black felt-tip markers
- water-based markers (red, orange, yellow, and brown)
- 12-by-18-inch white construction paper

Directions

Have students:

1. With a pencil draw a leaf, with veins, on a 3-by-3-inch square of paper, filling the entire paper.

2. Place the 3-by-3-inch paper on top of the Styrofoam square. Trace the leaf onto the Styrofoam by pressing firmly with the pencil to make indentations on the Styrofoam. Trace the veins.

3. Cut out the Styrofoam leaf.

4. At a window, light source (i.e., light table), or with carbon paper, transfer the leaf onto 12-by-18-inch white construction paper with a black felt-tip marker in a repeating design. All leaves should touch.

5. Plan a repeating "fall" color scheme using red, orange, yellow, or brown. Use water-based markers to "ink" the Styrofoam leaf. Press the inked leaf onto the paper inside the traced leaf shapes. Print a repeating design using alternating colors.

Design Element: Composition—repetition; Area—silhouette shapes; Color—fall colors

Art History: Warhol for repetition

Grade Level: Intermediate

Materials

- 9-by-12-inch white drawing paper
- wide-tip markers (including black)
- ruler
- pencil

Directions

Have students:

1. On a 9-by-12-inch paper, mark off every 3 inches on the two 9-inch edges. Connect opposite marks with horizontal lines—the two horizontal lines will divide the paper into thirds.

2. Turn the paper so the long side is horizontal. Using capital letters, have students write their first name so that the letters touch and fill the entire top row, making the letters the same width. Students may have to make a short name stretch out or make a long name with skinny letters.

3. Have students write their middle name the same way in the middle row, trying to make the letters the same width.

4. Have students write their last name the same way in the bottom row, trying to make the letters the same width.

5. Trace over letters with the wide side of a black marker.

6. Using markers, color in the background shapes with analogous colors.

Design Element: Composition—asymmetrical balance; Color—analogous colors
Art History: Piet Mondrian for asymmetrical balance
Grade Level: Intermediate

Materials

- three sheets of 4-by-6-inch tagboard
- 12-by-18-inch tagboard
- oil pastels
- black tempera paint, slightly diluted
- optional: X-ACTO Knife*
- hole punch
- large paintbrush
- yarn, any color
- pencil
- visual references of images and patterns used on Navajo blankets

Directions

Have students:

1. On one 4-by-6-inch tagboard, draw one Navajo blanket pattern. Repeat with a different design on the two remaining 4-by-6-inch tagboards.

2. Shade the back of each blanket pattern with pencil to make "carbon paper," or cut pattern from tagboard to create a template. Some interior shapes may need to be precut with an X-ACTO knife.

3. At a window, light source (i.e., light table), or with carbon paper, transfer one blanket design repeatedly down the center of 12-by-18-inch tagboard, from top to bottom.

4. Trace the two remaining blanket designs, one on either side of the first design, from top to bottom.

5. Color the shapes and background with oil pastels. Leave a gap between each color (the colors should not touch).

6. Apply one coat of slightly diluted black tempera paint with a large paintbrush.

7. On the 12-inch edge of the tagboard, use a hole punch to make holes approximately ½ inch from the edge, and 1 inch apart. Thread a 6-inch long piece of yarn through each hole and tie in a knot.

Design Element: Composition—symmetry with repetition

Art History: Navajo blankets for symmetry and repetition

Grade Level: Intermediate

*Review with students safety precautions in handling sharp blades. Cut away from your hand.
Do not walk around with the knife. Have cardboard underneath. Do not talk while cutting. Knives are not toys.

Materials

- 2-by-3-inch tagboard
- 9-by-12-inch paper
- 9-by-12-inch white drawing paper
- markers, all colors
- scissors
- pencil

Directions

Have students:

1. On 2-by-3-inch tagboard, have students draw their initials in block letters. Make sure that the letters touch the edges of the tagboard and each other.

2. Cut out so the initials remain connected.

3. Make three practice repeating designs on 9-by-12-inch paper. Students can "flip-flop" the initial template by tracing it right side up and then flip it over so the initials are reversed. Vary each design.

4. Choose one design and draw on 9-by-12-inch drawing paper.

5. Outline the design with black marker.

6. Color the design with three analogous colors of marker.

Design Element: Composition—repetition

Art History: Warhol for repetition

Grade Level: Intermediate

Materials

- visual references of African masks
- 12-by-18-inch tagboard
- oil pastels (yellow, gold, orange, and red)
- black tempera paint, slightly diluted
- paintbrush
- jute
- hole punch
- pencil
- scissors
- stapler

Directions

Have students:

1. On 12-by-18-inch tagboard, draw an oval shape for a mask.

2. Draw a *T* that will lay out the placement of the eyes, nose, and mouth.

3. On the *T*, draw in shapes to create stylized—simplified—eyes, a nose, and a mouth.

4. With yellow, gold, orange, or red oil pastel, draw lines that repeat the shapes of the eyes, nose, and mouth. Leave a space between each line. The lines should not cross the *T*. (See example.)

5. Repeat step 4 until the entire mask is filled with the same color or various colors.

6. Apply one coat of slightly diluted black tempera paint to the mask.

7. With a hole punch, make holes around the edge of the mask wherever hair is desired.

8. Tie on jute and fray.

9. To make three-dimensional, cut in about three inches at the four compass points. Overlap the flaps created by the cuts and staple together.

Design Element: Composition—symmetry

Art History: African masks for symmetry

Grade Level: Intermediate

Repetition of Positive and Negative Shapes

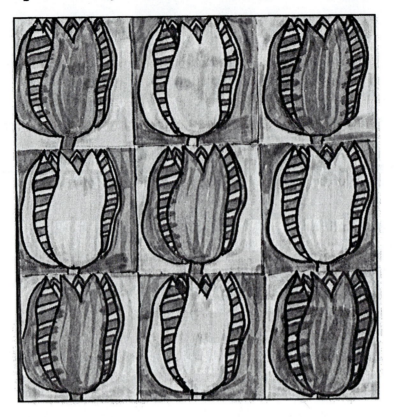

Materials

- yucca pods or any flower, vegetable, or fruit for visual reference
- ruler
- 3-by-3-inch paper
- 9-by-9-inch white drawing paper
- markers, all colors
- fine-point felt-tip pen
- pencil
- optional: carbon paper

Directions

Have students:

1. Inside a 3-by-3-inch square of paper, draw a yucca pod that touches all four edges of the paper.

2. Measure off a 3-by-3-inch grid on a sheet of 9-by-9-inch paper.

3. With pencil, shade the back of the 3-by-3-inch paper with the yucca pod drawing (or use carbon paper).

4. Trace the drawing into each 3-by-3-inch square (the same way each time).

5. Choose two colors of marker.

6. In the first square, color the yucca pod one color and the background the second color (e.g., red for the pod and yellow for the background).

7. Reverse the colors in the next box.

8. Continue coloring as in steps 6–7.

9. Outline each yucca pod with a fine-point felt-tip marker.

Design Element: Composition—repetition; Area—positive and negative shapes

Art History: Warhol for repetition

Grade Level: Intermediate

Materials

- 4-by-4-inch paper
- 12-by-16-inch white drawing paper
- ruler
- markers, all colors
- pencil
- optional: carbon paper

Directions

Have students:

1. Mark off every ½ inch (all edges) around a 4-by-4-inch square of paper and number the marks (including the corners) 1–8 on each side, starting at the top left corner. The number at the top right corner will be a 1 (starting at the right side).

2. Circle the numbers 4 and 5 on each side.

3. Draw a line in any fashion from 5 on the top edge to 4 on the right edge.

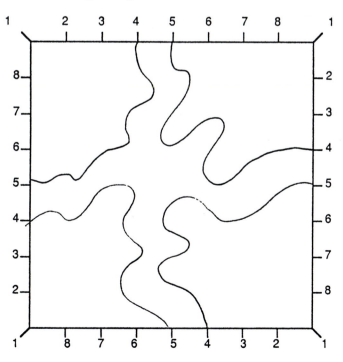

4. Draw a line from 5 on the right edge to 4 on the bottom edge. The line must initially follow the first line (see the example on page 31).

5. Repeat step 4 for the two remaining sets of 5s and 4s.

6. From 6 to 3 on each side, draw a line that follows the lines drawn from 5 to 4. Repeat from 7 to 2 and 8 to 1 on each edge.

7. Mark off a grid of 4-by-4-inch squares on 12-by-16-inch drawing paper.

8. At a window, light source (i.e., light table), or with carbon paper, transfer the design into each square, but turn it differently each time. The lines along the edges of each square must line up.

9. Trace over the lines with black marker. Using markers, color between one set of lines using one color and the neighboring space between two lines with a second color. Repeat this alternating pattern until all spaces are colored.

Design Element: Composition—repetition
Art History: Moorish tile design; Warhol for repetition
Grade Level: Intermediate

Materials

- visual references of Victorian architecture
- 12-by-18-inch tagboard
- ruler
- black felt-tip pen
- color pencils
- scissors
- pencil

Directions

Have students:

1. On 12-by-18-inch tagboard, mark off a 1-inch wide band 4 inches from the bottom 12-inch edge of the paper. Score and fold on the lines as shown in the illustration.

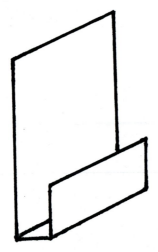

2. On the large section above the 1-inch band, draw an asymmetrical Victorian house that shows symmetrical architectural parts.

3. On the reverse side of the paper (with 4-inch portion folded up), draw a Victorian person, car, or carriage in the 4-inch wide section. Use the bottom edge at the fold as the base of the figure. Draw the person, car, or carriage as tall as the 4-inch section of the paper.

4. Outline the house and Victorian person, car, or carriage with a black felt-tip pen. Color with color pencils, using at least four colors.

5. Cut out carefully around the house, person, car, or carriage and the 1-inch band so all remain connected.

6. Fold the two sides so that the person, car, or carriage appears to be in front of the house.

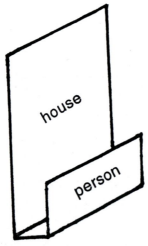

Design Element: Composition—asymmetrical design with symmetrical components

Art History: Victorian architecture for asymmetry and symmetry

Grade Level: Intermediate

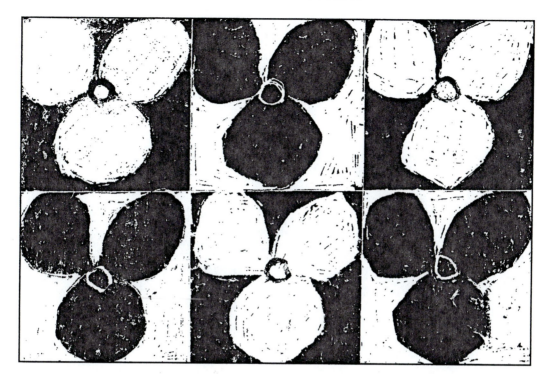

Materials

- plastic flowers for visual reference
- 3-by-3-inch paper
- 6-by-9-inch tagboard
- stylus or pointed wooden skewer
- crayons
- ruler

Directions

Have students:

1. Color white sheet of 6-by-9-inch tagboard completely with any colors of crayon in any shapes desired. Color very hard.

2. Color over all the shapes with black crayon. Color very hard.

3. Mark off a grid of 3-by-3-inch squares on the 6-by-9-inch tagboard.

4. Connect the marks using a ruler and a stylus.

5. Using a plastic flower as a reference, draw a flower on the 3-by-3-inch square. Make sure the flower touches all four edges of the square.

6. At a window, light source (i.e., light table), or with carbon paper, transfer the flower into each square on the 6-by-9-inch tagboard.

7. Using a stylus, "scratch out" the flower in the first square, the background in the next square. Repeat in this alternating fashion.

Design Element: Composition—repetition; Area—positive and negative shapes

Art History: Warhol for repetition

Grade Level: Intermediate

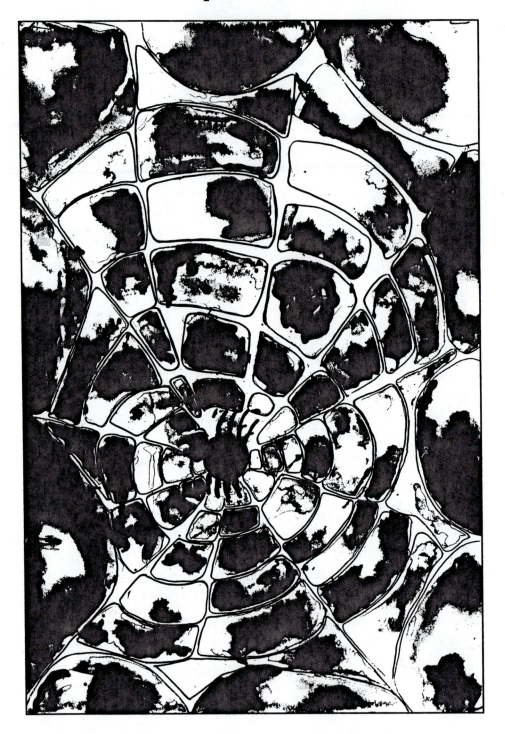

Materials

- 12-by-18-inch tagboard
- white oil pastel
- watercolor paints

- pencil
- optional: felt-tip markers

Directions

Have students:

1. On 12-by-18-inch tagboard, use a pencil to draw a radial spider web design. Make sure the web touches all four edges of the paper. Start with "support bars," which are the lines from the center of the web to the edges of the paper. Then draw the web lines between the "support bars."

2. At a window, light source (i.e., light table), or with carbon paper, transfer the spider web design onto the backside of the tagboard at a window or a light source using a white oil pastel.

3. Choose three analogous colors of watercolor paint.

4. Brush water into each background shape, that is, the shapes between the white web lines, and paint with watercolor paints using one, two, or, all three analogous colors. The colors will "bleed" together and the paint will not stick to the oil pastel.

5. A spider may be added using felt-tip markers.

Design Element: Composition—radial
Art History: Gothic rose window for radial composition
Grade Level: Intermediate

Materials

- 12-by-18-inch white construction paper
- any three colors of markers and a black marker
- visual references of letter fonts
- pencil

Directions

Have students:

1. On 12-by-18-inch white construction paper, use a pencil to draw 10 wavy lines lengthwise across the paper.

2. Choose any three colors of markers and a black marker.

3. In every other space between the lines, have students write their name. Use a different style or font of letter in each space and the three colors of markers and a black marker.

4. In the remaining spaces between lines, draw a different type of line design for each space. With the three colors of marker and a black marker try to use as much of each color and black in the overall composition to maintain color balance. The white of the paper may be considered an additional color if the student so decides.

Design Elements: Composition—repetition; Line—line variety

Art History: Picasso for line variety

Grade Level: Intermediate

Materials

- 12-by-18-inch tagboard
- oil pastels (white, light blue, blue, violet, and gray)
- black tempera paint, slightly diluted
- paintbrush
- pencil
- ruler

Directions

Have students:

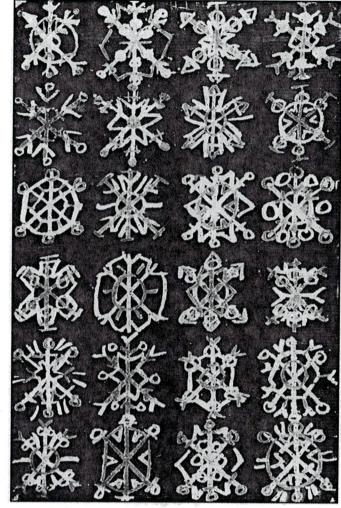

1. On 12-by-18-inch tagboard, mark off a grid of 3-by-3-inch squares.

2. Using white, light blue, blue, violet, and gray oil pastels, make a fat *X* with a vertical line down through the center in each square. Do not make the X lines go to the corners of the square. Alternate the colors of the *X* in each square.

3. Using *O*'s, *V*'s, and short straight lines, draw a design on one arm of a snowflake. Repeat the design on the five remaining arms of the snowflake. Add other radial designs as desired. Use white, light blue, blue, violet, and gray oil pastel.

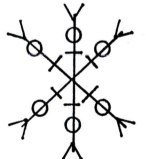

4. Repeat step 3 for each snowflake, using different combinations of lines and colors.

5. Apply one coat of slightly diluted black tempera paint to the entire paper. The black tempera paint should not adhere to the oil pastel.

Design Element: Composition—repetition, radial

Art History: Warhol for repetition

Grade Level: Upper elementary

Materials

- visual references of Aztec relief carvings
- 3-by-3-inch paper
- 3-by-3-inch Styrofoam
- 6-by-9-inch piece of grocery bag
- black printers ink
- brayer (for rolling out ink on a flat surface such as a piece of plexiglass)
- plexiglass sheet at least 3 by 9 inches (or a formica table top)
- tape

Directions

Have students:

1. On 3-by-3-inch paper, draw a symmetrical Aztec design. Be sure your design touches all four edges of the paper.

2. Tape the design onto 3-by-3-inch Styrofoam and using a blunt pencil, depress the areas that you do *not* want to print. Use short strokes to depress an area. (Raised areas will print.)

3. Wet a piece of 6-by-9-inch grocery bag and gently squeeze or wad and re-wad until bag becomes soft.

4. Let the grocery bag dry.

5. Squirt a dime-size pile of printer's ink onto plexiglass.

6. Roll out the paint using the brayer.

7. With the ink on the brayer, roll the brayer over the Styrofoam.

8. Using the inked Styrofoam, start at the top left corner of the 6-by-9-inch grocery bag, print the Aztec design in a repeating design over the entire surface of the bag. Edges of prints should touch but not overlap.

Design Element: Composition—repetition, symmetry

Art History: Aztec relief carvings for repetition and symmetry

Grade Level: Upper elementary

Materials

- 8-by-10-inch paper
- 8-by-10-inch corrugated cardboard
- 8-by-10-inch construction paper (enough for 3 prints by each student)
- carbon paper
- X-ACTO knife*

- brayer
- water-based printer's ink, any color
- plexiglass sheet at least 3 by 9 inches
- pencil
- carbon paper

Directions

Have students:

1. On 8-by-10-inch paper, draw a balanced asymmetrical design of three circles, three triangles, and three squares. Make sure that some object touches each of the four edges of the paper.

2. At a window, light source (i.e., light table), or with carbon paper, transfer the design onto 8-by-10-inch corrugated cardboard.

3. Decide which shapes should be cut out completely, which shapes should have the top layer of paper removed, and which shapes remain as they are. Maintain a balanced asymmetrical composition of the various surfaces.

4. Cut the cardboard according to plan from step 3, using an X-ACTO knife.

5. Squirt a dime-size pile of printer's ink onto plexiglass (for each printing).

6. Roll out the paint using the brayer.

7. With the ink on the brayer, roll the brayer onto the cardboard.

8. Print to the construction paper by pressing the inked cardboard onto the paper (make three prints). Save the best print.

Design Element: Composition—asymmetrical balance

Art History: Picasso for asymmetrical composition

Grade Level: Upper elementary

*Review with students safety precautions using knives. Cut away from your hand. Do not walk around with the knife. Have cardboard underneath. Do not talk while cutting.

Materials

- 12-by-18-inch white construction paper
- visual references of different fonts of letters
- felt-tip markers
- ruler
- pencil

Directions

Have students:

1. On 12-by-18-inch construction paper, mark off a 3-by-3-inch grid of squares.

2. In each square have students use a pencil to draw the first letter of their last name, using marker in a different style or font.

4. With markers, color each square differently with black, white, and any two other colors. (White is the white of the paper.) Some squares may have solid shapes of colors and some may have line designs. No two squares should be the same.

Design Element: Composition—repetition with unity and variety

Art History: Warhol for repetition

Grade Level: Upper elementary

Materials

- hand out a 1/8 of a circle pie-shape (6-inch-radius)
- 12-inch-diameter cardboard circle template with 1/8 pie divisions marked
- wide-tip markers (including black)
- 12-by-18-inch white drawing paper
- pencil
- tape
- scissors

Directions

Have students:

1. On the pie shape, have students write their names in pencil so that it touches the edges.

2. At a window, light source (i.e., light table), or with carbon paper, transfer the name with black marker, on the front side and back side.

3. Shade both sides of the pie shape with pencil, shading only the letters.

4. Cut out 1/8 pie shape.

5. Trace the circle template including the 1/8 pie division onto 12-by-18-inch white paper.

6. Tape the 1/8 pie-shaped name design in one of the 1/8 pie divisions on the 12-by-18-inch paper. Flip over the paper and use a pencil to trace the letters of the name and not the edges of the 1/8 pie shape. (The back side, without the pie divisions, becomes the front side.)

7. Reverse the name, tape, and trace it into the adjacent pie division.

8. Repeat step 7, reversing the name in each pie shape in an alternating fashion around the circle.

9. Trace the letters using the wide side of a black marker.

10. Color the spaces between the letters with analogous colors.

11. Cut out the circle.

Design Element: Composition—radial; Color—analogous colors

Art History: Gothic rose window for radial composition

Grade Level: Upper elementary

Materials

- hand out with a 1/8 of a circle pie-shaped paper (6-inch-radius)
- 12-by-18-inch white construction paper
- black permanent marker
- 12-inch-diameter cardboard circle template with 1/8 pie divisions marked
- watercolor paint
- paintbrush
- scissors
- pencil
- tape

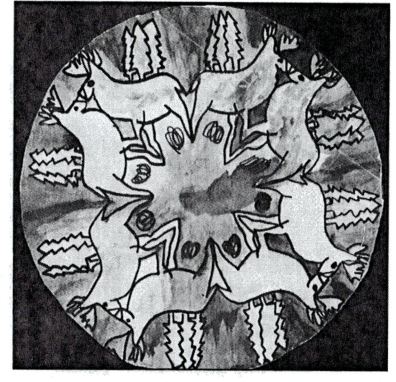

Directions

Have students:

1. Using pencil, draw an animal in the pie shape. The design must touch edges of the pie shape.

2. At a window, light source (i.e., light table), or with carbon paper, transfer the design with black marker, on the front side and back side.

3. Shade the lines of the design on both sides of the pie shape with pencil.

4. Cut out 1/8 pie shape.

5. Tape the 1/8 pie shape design in one of the 1/8 pie divisions on the 12-by-18-inch paper. Flip over the paper and use a pencil to trace the animal and not the edges of the 1/8 pie shape. (The back side, without the pie divisions, becomes the front side.)

6. Reverse the design, tape and trace it into the adjacent pie division.

7. Repeat step 6, reversing the design in each pie shape in an alternating fashion around the circle.

8. Outline the design with black permanent marker.

9. Paint the design with watercolor.

Design Element: Composition—radial

Art History: Gothic rose window for radial composition

Grade Level: Upper elementary

Materials

- 12-by-16-inch watercolor paper
- 2-inch-diameter circle template
- equilateral triangle template, with 2-inch apex
- watercolor paint
- ruler
- felt-tip black pen
- pencil

Directions

Have students:

1. On 12-by-16-inch water-color paper, mark off a grid of 4-by-4-inch squares.

2. In each square, use pencil to draw two circles, two triangles, and two one-inch wide straight stripes (the stripes can be horizontal, vertical, or diagonal, and should extend to the edges of the square). Circles and triangles should be drawn as if transparent—they may overlap each other showing the resulting overlap shapes. The stripes should be drawn to appear behind the circles and triangles.

3. Using watercolor paint, paint two objects one color, two objects a second color, and two objects a third color. All stripes and all transparent overlapping shapes of circles and squares together count as two objects (i.e., all striped and overlapping areas should be the same color). With complex overlaps, that is, when more than two circles and triangles overlap, paint every other shape. Try not to have two of the same color shapes side by side (they may, however, touch at corners).

4. Outline all shapes and grid lines with a felt-tip black pen. Use a ruler to make straight lines.

Design Element: Composition—asymmetry, repetition, unity with variety

Art History: Vasarely for asymmetry with repetition

Grade Level: Upper elementary

Materials

- 12-by-18-inch paper
- felt-tip black marker
- 18-by-24-inch black construction paper (or the design may be created on 9-by-12-inch paper and at a window, light source (i.e., light table), or with carbon paper, transfer to 12-by-18-inch paper)
- tissue paper (white, light blue, blue, and violet)
- scissors
- X-ACTO knife*
- stapler
- glue

Directions

Have students:

1. Using pencil on 12-by-18-inch paper, design a radial snowflake that has six "arms" (see figure below).

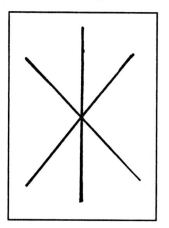

2. Using pencil, draw triangles, *V*'s, and *X*'s on one arm of the snowflake. Repeat the design on each arm of the snowflake.

3. With black marker, enlarge the lines so that they are ½-inch thick.

*Review with students safety precautions in using knives. Cut away from your hand. Do not walk around with the knife. Have cardboard underneath. Do not talk while cutting. Knives are not toys.

4. With black marker, design "supports" (similar to lead in stained glass), that extend from the edge of the snowflake to the edge of the paper. Each line should either be perpendicular to the edge of the paper or should extend diagonally to the corners of the paper. With black marker, make the edge of the paper a ½-inch-thick border.

5. Fold an 18-by-24-inch sheet of black construction paper to 12-by-18 inches and staple the design on top.

6. Cut out the negative areas, that is, the spaces between support bars and border with an X-ACTO knife. Cut through practice design and both layers of construction paper.

7. Remove 12-by-18-inch paper, open folded construction paper.

8. On one interior side, cut the tissue to fill the negative area spaces between the support bars. Cut tissue slightly larger than the negative area spaces to allow for gluing the tissue on the support bars. Cut and glue tissue for one space at a time.

9. On the "support" bars on the opposite interior side, place small dots of glue. Refold to original 12-by-18-inch size to seal the tissue paper between the two halves.

Design Element: Composition—radial

Art History: Gothic stained glass for radial composition

Grade Level: Upper elementary

Materials

- 4-by-4-inch paper with dots marked in ½-inch grid pattern (see figure below)
- 16-by-16-inch white paper
- felt-tip markers, all colors
- black felt-tip pen
- pencil

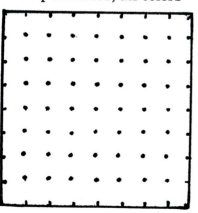

Directions

Have students:

1. On 4-by-4-inch paper, have students use a pencil to draw one initial from their first or last name. Write a cursive letter that uses the dots on the 4-by-4-inch grid. (See darkened lines of a cursive italicized D in figure below.)

2. Using pencil, make lines through the remaining dots as shown by the thin lines in the figure above. With a black felt-tip marker darken the lines on the back side of the paper (for easier tracing).

3. On 16-by-16-inch white paper, mark off a 4-by-4-inch grid

4. At a window, light source (i.e., light table), or with carbon paper, transfer the line design created in steps 1 and 2 into the first box of the 4-by-4-inch grid.

5. Reverse the pattern by flipping it over to the right and trace it into the next box in the first row. Flip the pattern to the right again and trace for the third box. Flip and trace again for the fourth box in the first row.

6. For the last box of the second row, "flip" down the pattern (reversing pattern from the above box) and trace. Flip the pattern to the left and trace for the third, second, and first boxes of the second row.

7. Complete the final two rows in a similar fashion (flip down and flip to the right for the third row; flip down and flip to the left for the fourth row). Adjacent squares will be mirror images to each other both vertically and horizontally.

8. Darken the lines with a black felt-tip pen.

9. Use markers to color between the lines, but do not color up to the lines—leave a white gap. Color repeating shapes the same color.

Design Element: Composition—repetition

Art History: Celtic manuscript illumination for repetition

Grade Level: Upper elementary

Materials

- visual references of Chilkat blankets from the Northwest Coast Native Americans, Tlingit Tribe
- 12-by-18-inch drawing paper
- 12-by-18-inch watercolor paper
- Chilkat-blanket-shaped template
- watercolor paint
- paintbrush
- black felt-tip pen
- hole punch
- scissors
- black, blue, and yellow yarn
- pencil
- 12-by-18-inch gray construction paper

Directions

Have students:

1. Using pencil, center and trace the blanket template onto 12-by-18-inch drawing paper. Find the center and draw a vertical line that divides the paper (and the blanket) in half.

2. Draw 10–12 Chilkat designs on one side of the blanket. Leave the same distance between each shape (this will create a "figure within a figure" design that is characteristic of the Chilkat blankets).

3. Fold the drawing paper in half along the center vertical line with the design on the outside, and at a window, light source (i.e., light table), or with carbon paper, transfer the reversed design onto the other·side to make a full-page symmetrical design.

4. Unfold, then trace the design onto watercolor paper.

5. Paint the design using black, diluted black, diluted blue, and diluted yellow watercolor paint. Make the colors symmetrical.

6. Outline the shapes with a black felt-tip pen.

7. Draw two black lines around the outside of the blanket shape.

8. Cut out the design.

9. Along the bottom of the blanket, between the two outer lines, use a hole punch to make a hole every inch.

10. Tie 6-inch black, yellow, and/or blue yarn into the holes to make a fringe (the fringe may be all one color or arranged in some type of color pattern).

11. Glue the design onto gray construction paper (gray construction paper makes an attractive project).

Design Element: Composition—symmetry

Art History: Chilkat blankets, Tlingit Tribe for symmetry

Grade Level: Upper elementary

Chapter

2

Line

The groundwork for any art project incorporates the basic design element of *line*. Line is the primary tool that the artist manipulates to represent his or her world. No matter what medium or media will be used, the artist first plans the composition by reducing the subject matter to a line or lines. Using lines, the artist renders three-dimensional objects on a two-dimensional surface—not an easy task for the beginning art student.

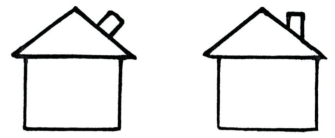

The teacher's task and the student's challenge involves training the eye to view a three-dimensional world in a two-dimensional manner so that the subject matter can be drawn with lines on a flat surface. The student must learn to look at objects in a new way, so as to draw what is seen, not the student's perception of what is seen. For example, a student might draw a chimney on the roof of a house so that the chimney appears to be at a 45-degree angle to the rest of the house.

The student has drawn the chimney perpendicular to the angle of the roof and not to the horizon line or the base of the house. The student needs to look at the lines of the chimney, in this case the side of the chimney, to determine what other lines of the house match the lines of the chimney. The student will see that the lines of the side of the chimney are the same as the lines of the side of the house. In this manner, the student begins to view a three-dimensional object as two-dimensional.

Another interesting aspect of line comes with the realization that line does not actually exist in nature. As an illustration, to draw a corner of a room the student will use a vertical line with a V at the top and an inverted V at the bottom. The student is actually drawing two walls, a ceiling, and a floor that meet. These surfaces meet to form corners. An artist uses lines to represent the meeting of these planes that create corners. Another example can be found in a portrait drawing. To show the jaw and the chin, the artist uses a U-shaped line. In reality, the jaw and the chin are made up of one continuous surface. If the student runs his hand from his cheek, down his jaw and to his neck, he will realize that his face is one continuous surface. An artist uses a line to show the contour of the jaw and chin. The student should understand that an artist uses line to show an illusion of the surfaces, edges, and planes of the subject matter.

Objective, Subjective, and Non-Objective Use of Line

As discussed in chapter 1, "Composition," a student may render the subject matter in an *objective*, *subjective*, or *non-representational* manner. Using line, the subject matter can be drawn realistically, abstractly, or non-objectively.

With an *objective* use of line, the student uses lines to draw the subject matter as realistically as possible. The lines may portray not only the contour edges of the subject matter but also the values and textures. Albrecht Dürer's wood-block print *The Four Horsemen of the Apocalypse* is an excellent example of the objective use of line.

With a *subjective* use of line, the student uses lines to simplify, abstract, or distort the subject matter. However, the subject matter is still recognizable. Georges Rouault's *The Old King* shows the artist's use of bold black lines to outline the various contour edges around and within his subject matter; however, the viewer still recognizes the lines as portraying a king.

With a *non-representational* use of line, the student does not represent any recognizable objects but instead uses lines to represent some type of *movement, character, emotion*, or *decoration*. The Op Art of Bridget Riley incorporates lines to create the optical illusion of *movement*. The lines are placed so that the surface appears to vibrate. The drawings of Honore Daumier show how lines can capture the **movement** of a figure. Daumier's *The Clown* is a fine example. The multitude and variety of lines in Willem de Kooning's *Woman VI* portray *character*. In this case, the tension created by the lines results in a sinister portrayal of the subject matter's character. The bold, jagged black lines in Franz Kline's *Mahoning* portray *emotion*. The size of Kline's work (6 feet 8 inches by 8 feet 4 inches) enhances the emotional effect evoked by the massive, angular lines. Even though Jean Dubuffet is known for his highly textured paintings, he also shows how lines can be used for *decoration* of a surface. Dubuffet's *Nunc Stans* is filled with both curvilinear and straight lines that result in a richly decorated picture plane.

As the various art history examples show, lines can be any width and length. Lines can be curved, straight, angular, or a combination of the aforementioned lines. The artist chooses to draw the subject matter using a type of line that will make visual his or her thoughts and perceptions of the world. Henri de Toulouse-Lautrec's *Jane Avril* provides an excellent example of how an artist can manipulate the width of a line, referred to as a *calligraphic* line, to capture the contour of a figure.

Line and Other Design Elements

The study of line in and of itself offers many possibilities for art projects. However, line is also the basic foundation for the design elements of *area, value, texture, color,* and *space*. Line should not be considered less important than the other design elements, but as a familiar friend that introduces the student to new opportunities for study.

For example, line can be used to show the *area* or shape of an object. The artist shows the contour edges with a line. Tracing one's hand provides simple illustration of how a contour line shows the shape of the hand. Joan Miró's *Composition* contains lines that show very simplified shapes of figures.

Lines may be any *value* of black. By applying different pressures while drawing with a pencil or by using pencils with varying degrees of hard and soft lead, the student will discover the added possibilities that value can add to the character of line. *The Descent from the Cross: By Torchlight* by Rembrandt Van Rijn contains lines of various value that add to the drama of the scene.

Line is a component of *texture* by means of the artist's use of various lines to represent texture. The artist's eye analyzes the surface of an object in terms of what type of lines make up the texture. For example, thin parallel lines can portray the texture of a feather, whereas a series of closely spaced small dots can represent sand. Albrecht Dürer's *Self-Portrait* shows how lines can represent the texture of hair, fur, and cloth.

The study of line should not be limited to pencil or ink. The combination of line and *color* offers exciting possibilities, especially when exploring line variety or lines that portray texture. The Japanese haiku drawings combine calligraphic lines and colors to portray words and objects from nature with simplified, curving lines.

The illusion of *space* can be created by the way the artist arranges lines on the picture plane. A drawing of a sidewalk offers a simple example. Two lines are far apart at the bottom of the picture plane and are gradually closer together toward the top. These *converging parallel* lines thereby create the illusion of a receding sidewalk. The ceiling and the walls in Leonardo Da Vinci's *The Last Supper* show how lines can create the illusion of space.

Materials

- 9-by-24-inch (or 9-by-18-inch) white construction paper
- visual references of dinosaur bones
- color pencils or Caran D'Ache (water-soluble crayons)
- black wedge-tip marker
- black felt-tip pen
- paintbrush
- pencil

Directions

Have students:

1. Using pencil, draw wavy lines horizontally across the 9-inch width of the 9-by-24-inch construction paper.

2. Using pencil, draw grass on the top line (or draw whatever you think there will be on ground that covers dinosaur bones).

3. Draw dinosaur bones in three or four strata.

4. Outline the strata divisions with the wide side of a black marker.

5. Using color pencils or Caran D'Ache, draw a different variety of line in each stratum. Use two colors in each stratum. If Caran D'Ache are used, brush water over each stratum to blend the colors within that stratum.

6. Outline the line designs with a black felt-tip pen.

Design Element: Line—line variety

Art History: Picasso's Abstract Period for line variety

Grade Level: Lower primary

Fall Leaves
(monoprint using oil pastels)

Materials

- brown felt-tip marker
- 9-by-12-inch white and brown construction paper
- two 8-by-11-inch photocopy paper sheets, white or goldenrod
- scissors
- oil pastels (yellow, gold, orange, brown, and red)
- pencil
- glue
- tape

Directions

Have students:

1. On 8-inch-by-11-inch photocopy paper, draw one leaf so that it touches the top and bottom edges of the 8-inch paper.

2. Draw veins with two parallel lines.

3. On 9-by-12-inch white construction paper, draw a wiggle line that touches all four edges of the paper. (See "Symmetrical Butterfly" on page 6.)

4. Color each shape created by the wiggle line a different color with oil pastels. Do not use the color of the photocopy paper.

5. Tape the leaf drawing on top of the construction paper.

6. Using a pencil, make hatching lines, that is, five short lines in one direction within the leaf. Draw hatching lines in different directions until the entire leaf is filled. Do not fill in the vein spaces created by two parallel lines. Sets of hatching lines should not cross each other.

7. Remove the photocopy paper. The reverse side now has color hatching lines. On the color side, draw in the veins with a brown marker. Repeat previous steps for a second leaf.

8. Cut out the leaves and glue onto brown construction paper.

9. Using "fall" colors of oil pastel, that is, yellow, gold, orange, brown, and red, fill in the entire background of the brown construction paper with contour lines of the leaves.

Design Element: Line—line variety, contour lines, hatching lines; Color—fall colors

Art History: Albrecht Dürer for line variety

Grade Level: Lower primary

Materials

- 12-by-18-inch white construction paper
- markers (variety of colors)

Directions

Have students:

1. Hand out pre-drawn construction paper with students' names in "bubble letters," as shown.

2. Using marker, draw one kind of line around the name. Be sure to follow shape of name.

3. Draw another kind of line around the name, using a different color of marker.

4. Keep making different lines until the entire paper is filled (lines may begin to "run off" the edge of the paper).

5. Use any colors of marker to color lines and to color between the lines (new lines will be created without even thinking!).

Design Element: Line—line variety

Art History: Picasso's Abstract Period for line variety

Grade Level: Lower primary

Cut Lines with Lines

Materials

- 9-by-18-inch tagboard or manila paper
- 12-by-18-inch construction paper
- color pencils or crayons
- black marker
- scissors
- pencil

Directions

Have students:

1. To make a template, draw a wave line lengthwise across 9-by-18-inch tagboard or manila paper. Make sure line goes entirely across the paper and from top to bottom as well. The line should not touch the top or bottom edge.

2. Cut along the line.

3. Save one side of the paper and mark an *X* in the lower left corner to remember which side is the front side.

4. Trace the wave template along each edge of a sheet of 12-by-18-inch construction paper, that is, on all four edges. Be sure to line up the template on the edges of the paper and be sure that the *X* has been placed in each corner.

5. Outline the edge of the template with a black marker on the construction paper.

6. Using various colors of pencil, fill in each shape with a different kind of line.

Design Element: Line—line variety

Art History: Picasso's Abstract Period for line variety

Grade Level: Lower primary

Materials

- 6-by-18-inch watercolor paper
- masking tape
- watercolor paints
- 1-inch-wide watercolor paintbrush
- black felt-tip pen

Directions

Have students:

1. Tape 6-by-18-inch watercolor paper to the table along all four edges.

2. Brush water onto watercolor paper. Using water and then dark blue, blue, green, and dark green watercolor paint, paint long *S* lines the length of the paper (this is "wet on wet" watercolor technique). The *S* lines should follow each other. Use the wide side and the thin side of the paintbrush to make different *S*'s with varying line thicknesses.

3. Carefully pull off the masking tape, leaving a white border.

4. Using a black marker, draw large, medium, and small rocks. Make them touch and follow the *S* shapes. In dark green areas, make the rocks large. In blue areas, make the rocks medium. In green areas, make the rocks small. If you cannot tell the color of an area, leave it blank.

5. Color between the large and medium rocks with black marker.

Design Element: Line—movement

Art History: J. M. W. Turner for lines showing movement

Grade Level: Lower primary

Materials

- 4 sheets 4-by-6-inch construction paper, any color
- 12-by-18-inch construction paper, any color but the color of the 4-by-6-inch paper
- scissors
- glue
- pencil

Directions

Have students:

1. On 4-by-6-inch construction paper, draw a type of line from corner to corner diagonally.

2. On the remaining 4-by-6-inch pieces, draw either the same line or three more different types of lines from corner to corner.

3. Fold a 12-by-18-inch piece of construction paper in half once horizontally and once vertically so that creases are made that divide the paper into quarters.

4. Cut along the lines of the 4-by-6-inch pieces.

5. Glue one of the cut pieces of 4-by-6-inch paper into one of the corners of quarter shape. Glue the other cut piece into the corner that is at a diagonal. Repeat for remaining three quarter shapes. They may be arranged to create an X-shaped negative area, a diamond-shaped negative area, or a two V-shaped negative areas.

Design Element: Line—line variety, lines creating shapes

Art History: Matisse for cut-paper shapes

Grade Level: Lower primary and up

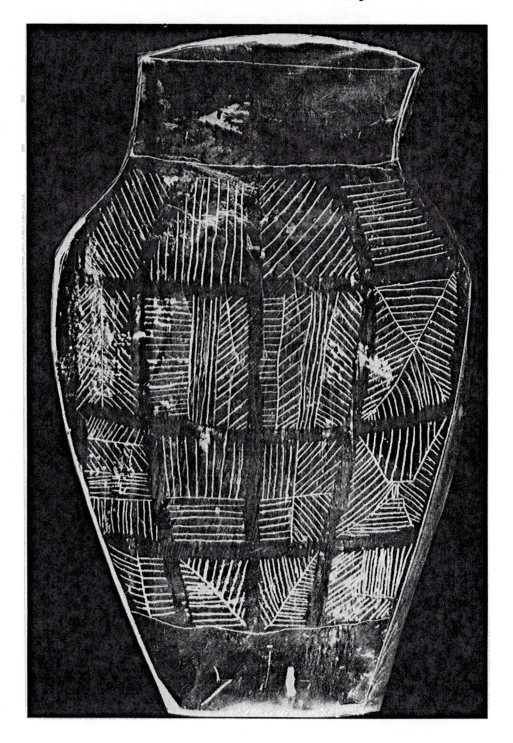

Materials

- Three 8-by-14-inch handouts with a different pottery shape on each.
- crayons
- India ink and black tempera mixture (this ink is permanent when spilled, have students bring in old shirts to wear when doing this project)
- paintbrush
- stylus, wooden sticks, or paper clips

- 12-by-18-inch tagboard
- 12-by-18-inch construction paper
- tape
- glue
- pencil
- scissors

Directions

Have students:

1. On sheets with pottery shapes, create a design in each box using the following hatching lines.

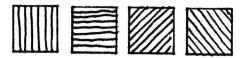

Students' lines may not cross! Use one design for one box. Each box should be a different design. Students may divide a box to have two, three, or four hatch lines.

2. On a 12-by-18-inch piece of tagboard, choose two of the following colors of crayons: yellow, gold, orange, or red. Color the entire page as solidly as possible. Give it a second coat of either the same color or one of the other three. No white paper should show.

3. Help students paint black ink and tempera mixture over the entire tagboard on the crayon side. Let dry.

4. Choose one pottery design. Tape the paper over the painted side of the tagboard and trace over the pot shape and boxes. Do not trace the line designs.

5. Remove the paper and scratch line designs in with small sticks or a paper clip. Do not outline the boxes.

7. Cut out the pot and glue on construction paper.

Design Element: Line—hatching lines

Art History: San Juan Pueblo Pottery for hatching lines

Grade Level: Intermediate

Materials

- 6-by-9-inch corrugated cardboard with top layer removed.
- X-ACTO knife*
- brayers
- plexiglass sheet or formica top
- printer's ink or tempera with liquid starch
- 6-by-9-inch construction paper
- pencil
- carbon paper

Directions

Have students:

1. On 6-by-9-inch paper, plan a design of either circles or squares. Make sure they do not overlap. The squares must be square.

2. Using carbon paper transfer design to cardboard that has had the top layer of paper peeled off. The ridges will be showing.

3. Cut out the shapes and place them back in the opening but make the ridges go in a different direction.

4. Squirt a dime-size pile of printer's ink onto plexiglass.

5. Roll out the ink using the brayer.

6. With the ink on the brayer, roll the brayer onto the card.

7. Place a piece of construction paper on top of card and rub it to pick up the ink.

Design Element: Line—hatching lines

Art History: Dürer's woodcut prints for prints with hatching lines

Grade Level: Intermediate

*Review with students safety precautions in using knives. Cut away from your hand. Do not walk around with the knife. Have cardboard underneath. Do not talk while cutting. Knives are not toys.

Crosshatch Tree

Materials

- 9-by-12-inch white drawing paper
- crayons
- India ink and black tempera mixture (this ink is permanent when spilled, have students bring in old shirts to wear when doing this project)
- stylus, wooden stick, or paper clip
- ruler
- pencil

Directions

Have students:

1. Draw a tree on white 9-by-12-inch paper. Make sure the branches and the trunk touch all edges of the paper.

2. With crayons, color the trunk brown and each negative area a different color. Do not use black.

3. Paint India ink and black tempera mixture over the entire surface. Let dry.

4. Using a ruler and stylus, scratch the four crosshatch lines, that is, vertical, horizontal, and the two diagonal lines, over the entire paper. To achieve the best look, the lines should be scratched as close together as possible.

Design Element: Line—crosshatching; Area—negative area

Art History: Dürer for crosshatching; Mondrian for negative area

Grade Level: Intermediate

Materials

- still-life objects
- extension cord for visual reference
- 12-by-18-inch practice paper
- 12-by-18-inch white drawing paper
- 12-by-18-inch construction paper
- black felt-tip pen and marker
- pencil
- scissors
- glue

Directions

Have students:

1. On 12-by-18-inch practice paper, draw three objects from the classroom. Something must touch each edge of the paper, and each object should be drawn over another object to show transparency.

2. In the "empty" spaces, draw an extension cord that will balance these areas.

3. At a window, light source (i.e., light table), or with carbon paper, transfer to 12-by-18-inch white drawing paper.

4. In each shape created where the objects overlapped, draw in a different type of line with felt-tip pen. Do not draw lines in background shapes but only on objects.

5. Outline the objects with a black felt-tip marker.

6. Cut out the objects and the extension cord and glue onto construction paper (place glue on the back of the drawing; do not lift up; rather, lay the construction paper on top).

Design Element: Line—line variety for decoration; Space—transparency

Art History: Picasso's *Portrait of a Young Girl* for line variety

Grade Level: Intermediate

Materials

- 6-by-9-inch practice paper with a wiggle line drawn on it
- 12-by-18-inch construction paper
- fine-point felt-tip pens
- pencil

Directions

Have students:

1. On practice paper, practice drawing U-shaped lines that follow the wiggle guide line, as shown in the illustration on the right.

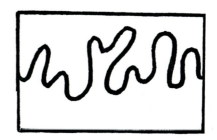

   The *U*'s must touch the guide line and the *U* above it. The *U*'s start out close together, then swing far apart, then close together again.

2. Once you are comfortable, start on 12-by-18-inch paper. With pencil, make sure your guide line covers the entire paper, but never crosses.

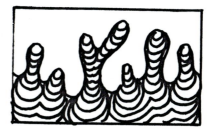

3. Use a fine-point felt-tip pen to make topographical lines on both sides of the guide line.

Design Element: Line—line showing depth

Art History: Bridget Riley for lines showing depth

Grade Level: Intermediate (great backup for teaching cursive strokes!)

Topographical Humans
(Mummy people!)

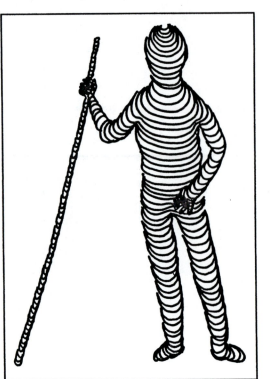

Materials

- magazine pictures of people
- ruler
- 9-by-12-inch practice paper
- 9-by-12-inch drawing paper
- 9-by-12-inch construction paper
- black felt-tip pen
- scissors
- glue
- construction paper
- pencil

Directions

Have students:

1. Choose a human figure from a magazine.

2. Mark off a ½-inch or 1-inch grid on the magazine figure.

3. Mark off a 1-inch or 2-inch grid on practice paper.

4. Draw lines and shapes of the figure on the paper. Be sure to notice how they cut through the grid lines.

5. Once drawn, transfer lines of the figure to 9-by-12-inch drawing paper at a window, light source (i.e., light table), or with carbon paper.

6. Fill in the shapes with topographical lines.

7. Cut out the figure and glue to any color of construction paper.

Design Element: Line—line showing depth

Art History: Bridget Riley for lines showing depth

Grade Level: Intermediate

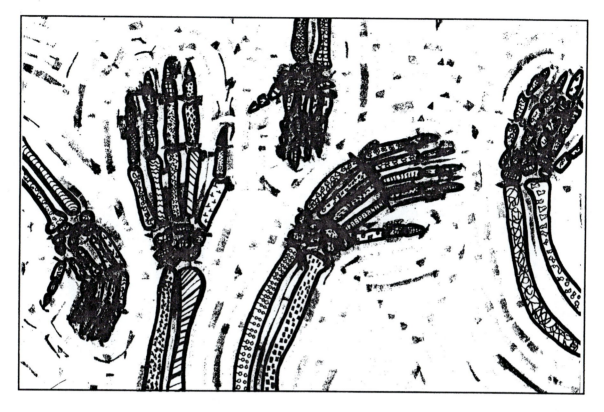

Materials

- 12-by-18-inch practice paper
- 12-by-18-inch white drawing paper
- visual references of hand bones or X-rays of hands
- color fine-point felt-tip pens
- color felt-tip markers
- markers
- pencil

Directions

Have students:

1. On 12-by-18-inch practice paper, draw five hands to create a balanced asymmetrical composition. Each hand must be in a different position.

2. Draw in the appropriate bones, in proportion and in scale.

3. At a window, light source (i.e., light table), or with carbon paper, transfer onto 12-by-18-inch white drawing paper with a fine-point felt-tip pen.

4. With fine-point felt-tip pen, fill in each bone shape with a different type of line design.

5. Using at least two different colors of marker, fill in the background with contour lines around the hands until the entire negative area is filled.

Design Element: Line—line variety, contour lines;
Area—proportion and scale

Art History: Picasso for line variety

Grade Level: Upper elementary

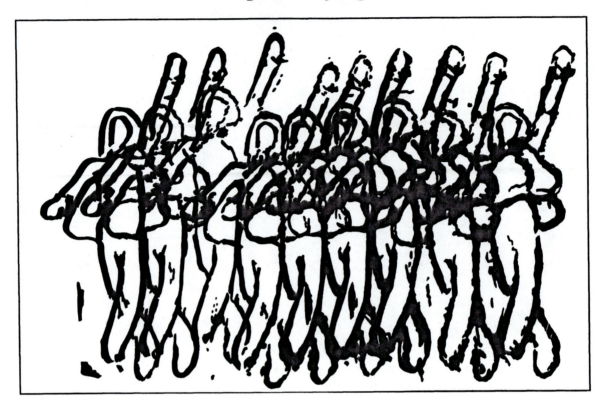

Materials

- magazine pictures of figures
- 9-by-12-inch practice paper
- 18-by-24-inch white construction paper
- 9-by-12-inch cardboard
- string
- ruler
- printer's ink, primary and secondary colors
- scissors
- brayers
- plexiglass sheet or formica top
- pencil
- glue

Directions

Have students:

1. Choose a magazine picture of a person showing the full body.

2. Mark off either a ½-inch or 1-inch grid over the figure.

3. Mark off a 1-inch or 2-inch grid on 9-by-12-inch practice paper.

4. Draw the edges of the figure as they go through each box of the grid. It is helpful to number each box across the top and down the left side of both the picture and the grid paper.

5. At a window, light source (i.e., light table), or with carbon paper, transfer lines of the figure, not the grid, onto cardboard.

6. Glue string onto lines.

7. Squirt a dime-size pile of printer's ink onto plexiglass.

8. Roll out the ink using the brayer.

9. With the ink on the brayer, roll the brayer onto the strings.

10. Turn over cardboard and place on white construction paper, press lightly to transfer ink.

11. Repeat steps 7–10 using analogous colors of printer's ink, print each color three times and overlap the figures by one-half each time.

Design Element: Line—contour lines; Color—analogous color; Space—movement through space

Art History: Giacomo Balla's *Dog Walking*; Marcel Duchamp's *Nude Descending a Staircase* for line showing movement

Grade Level: Upper elementary

Wind Tunnel

Materials

- 6-by-18-inch practice paper
- scraps of cardboard, tagboard, or mat board
- 6-by-18-inch cardboard
- string
- scissors
- 18-by-24-inch construction paper
- glue
- printer's ink
- 6-by-9-inch plexiglass
- brayers
- pencil

Directions

Have students:

1. On 6-by-18-inch practice paper, draw at least five geometric shapes.

2. With pencil, plan out how wind currents would go around these objects at a high rate of speed.

3. Once the teacher has approved, cut shapes from cardboard scraps.

4. Glue down the string with a solid bead of glue to show wind lines. Make sure the lines "flow" and are close together but never cross. Let dry overnight.

5. Mark the top of the cardboard on the back.

6. Squirt a dime-size pile of printer's ink onto plexiglass.

7. Roll out the ink using the brayer.

8. With the ink on the brayer, roll the brayer over the string and geometric shapes.

9. Print the design four times on 18-by-24-inch paper, alternating every other print by having the top of the cardboard at the bottom of the paper one time and at the top the next.

10. Repeat steps 6–9 with second color ink.

Design Element: Line—lines showing movement

Art History: Balla's *Dog Walking*; Duchamp's *Nude Descending a Staircase* for lines showing movement

Grade Level: Upper elementary

Materials

- yucca pods or any flower or plant for visual reference
- 12-by-18-inch practice paper

- 12-by-18-inch white drawing paper
- markers
- pencil

Directions

Have students:

1. On 12-by-18-inch practice paper, draw three yucca branches and six or more yucca pods. One branch should be drawn from the top edge of the paper to the bottom edge.

2. Transfer to 12-by-18-inch white drawing paper.

3. Color in the yucca branch and pod completely with black marker.

4. Choose three analogous colors of marker. Use these to outline the plant.

5. Keep repeating the three colors of contour lines in the negative area until the entire paper is filled.

Design Element: Line—contour lines; Area—silhouette shapes

Art History: Paul Klee's *Park Near Lucerne*; Edvard Munch's *The Scream* for contour lines

Grade Level: *Upper elementary*

Chapter
3
Area

The study of the design element of *area*, sometimes called shape, begins with training the eye to see the silhouette shape of an object, followed by the shapes within a object, and finally the shapes around the object. To understand the concept of silhouette shapes, the student simply needs to trace his or her hand, creating the outside shape with no interior shapes. A silhouette shape can also be described as the shadow shape of an object. If the student looks at a paint-by-number picture before it is painted, he or she will see how an object can be reduced to areas or shapes of colors within the silhouette shape. Once the student can see an object as a composition of shapes, he or she can draw anything. A helpful hint for the student involves looking at the geometric shapes or letter shapes, the *positive shapes*, that make up an object and the background shapes, the *negative shapes*, that surround an object. For example, the student might draw a window as a composition of positive and negative shapes. The positive shapes would be those that make up the window frame while the negative shapes would be the shape of the glass created by the positive shapes of the window frame.

If the student is aware of both the positive and negative shapes, a window can be shown two ways: by drawing the window frame or by drawing the shape of the glass. The student should understand that looking for both the positive and negative shapes that compose an object will allow greater ease with the drawing. Henri Matisse's *The Beasts of the Sea* shows how he uses both positive and negative shapes to show marine life.

Objective, Subjective, and Non-Representational Use of Area

As the student might expect, area may be used in an *objective*, *subjective*, or *non-representational* manner. Just as with line, the student may draw realistic shapes, abstracted shapes, or non-objective shapes. With each approach, the student must see a three-dimensional world in terms of two-dimensional shapes.

With an *objective* use of area, the student looks for the actual shapes that make up an object. The student may first concentrate on the silhouette shape of the object and then proceed to the shapes that make up the object. The shapes within the object may be areas of color, value, or texture. Henri Matisse's *Dance* is an example of the human figure reduced to a silhouette shape. The Photo Realist Audrey Flack's *Queen* portrays the shapes of color, value, and texture within a variety of objects.

With a **subjective** use of area, the student manipulates the shapes that are seen in an object. For example, the student might simplify an object by reducing the number of color shapes seen within it. The student might draw a face by using one color to show the light areas, a second color to show the medium-value areas, and a third color to show the dark areas. Roy Lichtenstein's *Whaam* is the artist's reduction of a jet fighter to three color shapes.

Changing the perceived areas to **biomorphic** or **geometric** shapes offers another subjective use of area. Biomorphic shapes are drawn using only curved lines, whereas geometric shapes are drawn using only straight lines. The Rococo artist Antoine Watteau used primarily biomorphic color shapes in *A Pilgrimage to Cythera*. Pablo Picasso's work from his Cubism period incorporates geometric shapes to represent the subject and its color shapes. Picasso's *Ambroise Vollard* is a reduction of objects to geometric shapes. Another interesting example of manipulating shapes can be found in the work of Fernand Léger. He reduced the human figures in *Three Women* to cylinder shapes.

With a **non-representational** use of area, the student uses shapes that do not portray any realistic object but rather unreal or fantasy shapes (i.e., imagined shapes). The student can observe how nondescriptive shapes have the ability to represent personality, character, and emotion. A comparison of the fluid color shapes in Paul Jenkins *Phenomena Astral Signal* to the geometric color shapes in Frank Stella's *Empress of India* affords the student an example of the various expressions that shapes can portray. The emotional effect of non-representational color shapes can be found in Willem De Koonnig's *Composition*. The work of the Surrealist Yves Tanguy incorporates fantasy shapes. Tanguy's *Multiplication of the Arcs* presents what appears to be a landscape filled with unrecognizable shapes.

Compositional Considerations

Areas (or shapes) of value, texture, and color comprise an important consideration for the **balance** of a composition. As discussed in chapter 1, "Composition," a well-balanced piece of art is one that has been based on the **principles of organization**. Likewise, shapes may be analyzed by the same guidelines. Namely, the shapes in a composition should have unity yet variety, rhythm and movement, proportion and scale, dominance and economy. All the shapes must work together to create a visually interesting yet balanced picture plane. Edward Hopper's *Early Sunday Morning* provides an excellent study of shapes that incorporate the principles of organization for a well-balanced picture plane.

Area and the Illusion of Space

The design element of area also provides the student an opportunity to create the illusion of **space**, or depth, on a two-dimensional surface. Chapter 7 is devoted to the design element of space; however, a simple illustration of how area can show space can be found in the drawing of a sidewalk leading up to a house.

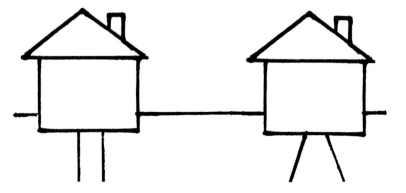

A student most likely will draw a sidewalk with parallel lines leading up to a front door because a sidewalk has a uniform width. In essence, the student might be tempted to draw the sidewalk as a tall, vertical rectangular shape. A tall, trapezoidal shape would be a more accurate representation of a sidewalk leading up to a house. The shape of the trapezoid creates the illusion of the sidewalk going off into space. Giorgio De Chirico's *The Mystery and Melancholy of a Street* is an example of how simple trapezoidal shapes create the illusion of depth. *The Story of Jacob and Esau* from Lorenzo Ghiberti's *Gates of Paradise* shows bas relief, an elaborate arrangement of shapes used to create an illusion of deep space on a shallow surface.

Area and Edges

Sometimes the discussion of area and shape leads the student to think there must be definite shapes to represent an object or a scene. However, the student should realize that an object can be composed of and/or surrounded by **hard edges** and **soft edges**. In a composition with hard edges, one color, value, or texture ends abruptly where another color, texture, or value begins. The student can see a "line" separating the two shapes. In a composition with soft edges, there is a subtle transition between the shapes of color, value, or texture that make up an object or between the object and the background. For an excellent example, the student can study Auguste Renoir's *Moulin de la Galette* to find that he filled his picture plane with hard and soft edges of colors within the clothing of the figures and the shadows in the background.

Patchwork Quilt

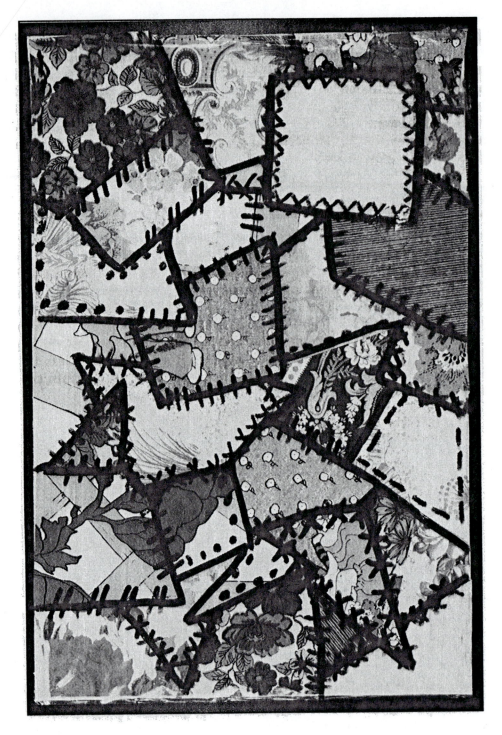

Materials

- wallpaper scraps
- 12-by-18-inch tagboard
- permanent markers
- scissors

- glue
- visual references of patchwork quilts, crazy quilts, and the varieties of stitches used

Directions

Have students:

1. On 12-by-18-inch tagboard, glue a variety of cut wallpaper shapes. Cut straight lines, but no squares. Make crazy shapes! Be sure that the wallpaper patterns have contrast in color and/or pattern. No white paper should be left showing.

2. Outline each shape with permanent black marker.

3. Using a permanent black marker, outline or draw across the edges of the shapes to show different kinds of stitches. Some examples are:

| | | | | | | XXXX   • • • •   +++++   - - - - -   \ \ \ \ \ \

Design Element: Area—geometric shapes; Line—line variety

Art History: Jean Dubuffet for variety of shapes

Grade Level: Lower elementary

Materials

- 12-by-18-inch construction paper, any color
- 12-by-18-inch black construction paper
- 12-by-18-inch practice paper
- 1-by-12-inch strips of construction paper for weaving, any color
- examples of animal faces from cartoon books
- scissors
- pencils
- glue
- ruler
- option, ¼-by-4-inch white strips

Directions

Have students:

1. Fold a 12-by-18-inch piece of construction paper in half widthwise so that each half then measures 9 by 12 inches.

2. Use a ruler to draw a line at the edge where the paper opens.

3. Draw seven different lines, or any number of lines, from the fold to the line at the edge of the paper.

4. Cut the lines while the paper is folded from the fold to the line at the edge.

5. Unfold and weave 1-by-12-inch strips of construction paper through the cut lines. If the first weave is "over then under," the next weave will be "under then over." Be sure that the woven strips are as close together as possible, that is, side by side.

6. Place a dot of glue under each strip so it does not slip.

7. Draw an animal face on a 12-by-18-inch practice paper, almost as large as the paper. Examples of animal faces from cartoon books are helpful.

8. Fold the practice paper in half lengthwise so that each half measures 6 by 18 inches. The animal face should be on the outside. Decide which half of the face is better. Place a folded piece of 12-by-18-inch black construction paper inside.

9. Cut along the outer contour edge of the animal face with paper still folded.

10. Glue down the negative area of the black construction paper, that is, the outside and not the face, on top of the weaving.

11. Make eyes, nose, and mouth from the positive shape, that is, the face shape. Option: Whiskers may be made from ¼-by-4-inch strips.

Design Element: Area—weaving lines, creating shapes, positive and negative shapes

Art History: Native American weavings; Matisse for positive and negative shapes

Grade Level: Lower primary

Materials

- 12-by-18-inch watercolor paper
- watercolor paints
- paintbrush
- black tempera paint or black construction paper
- scissors
- masking tape
- glue

Directions

Have students:

1. Tape all four edges of watercolor paper to the table.

2. With a brush, wet the entire paper.

3. Paint four wide bands of yellow with watercolor paint.

4. In between the yellow bands, paint orange using a circular movement. Start with large circular movements at the edge and end up small. Make sure to paint from edge to edge. There should be no white paper showing at this point (some yellow may be covered or overlapped with orange).

5. Paint red inside the orange bands using circular movement but smaller than the circular shapes of orange.

6. Paint a violet band at the bottom of the red band.

7. When the paper is dry, paint mesas and cactus with black tempera paint or cut out of black construction paper and glue onto watercolor paper.

Design Element: Area—hard and soft edges, silhouetted shapes

Art History: Turner for hard and soft edges

Grade Level: Lower primary

Materials

- 4-by-6-inch tagboard
- scissors
- chalk (red, orange, yellow, gold, brown, and two hues of green)
- 12-by-18-inch brown construction paper
- brown marker
- pencil

Directions

Have students:

1. Fold a 4-by-6-inch piece of tagboard in half.

2. Draw half a leaf. Be sure to have it touch the fold, but not the other three edges.

3. Cut out and save both pieces, that is, the leaf and the background. You now have two stencils, that is, the leaf is the positive shape while the background is the negative shape.

4. Choose three "fall" colors from red, orange, yellow, gold, and brown.

5. On 12-by-18-inch brown construction paper, use chalk to color off the edges of the two stencils. Use short and long strokes and then blend them with fingers. Do each color three times with each stencil. On the leaf, color off the edge. On the background, color into the shape. Use the entire paper so that it is asymmetrically balanced.

6. Color the background two hues of green and blend.

7. Outline the leaves and draw in the veins with a brown marker.

Design Element: Area—positive and negative shapes; Composition—asymmetrical balance

Art History: Matisse for positive and negative shapes

Grade Level: Lower primary

Materials

- 12-by-18-inch manila paper
- 12-by-18-inch black or blue or gray construction paper
- oil pastels (light pink, pink, light blue, blue, violet, and white)
- tape
- scissors
- 2-inch-diameter circle template
- pencil

Directions

Have students:

1. On 12-by-18-inch manila paper, draw three clouds. One of them must go across the entire paper. The other two should not.

2. Cut out and tape to colored construction paper.

3. Trace a circle (using the 2-inch template) anywhere on paper to make the moon. Color with white oil pastel.

4. Make rays from the moon that are short, close together, and overlapped. Use light pink, pink, light blue, blue, and finally violet in whatever order, but stay in a chosen order. Fill the entire paper and even color over the cloud shapes.

5. Remove manila paper for clouds so the clouds will appear to be the color of the construction paper.

6. Accent cloud edges closest to moon with white and light pink. Accent edges away from moon with blue and violet.

Design Element: Area—silhouette shapes

Art History: Vincent Van Gogh's *Starry Night*

Grade Level: Lower primary

Fish Tank

Materials

- 12-by-18-inch white drawing paper
- water-based markers
- paintbrushes
- thin black markers
- visual references of tropical fish and plants
- pencil

Directions

Have students:

1. On white paper, draw a fish as large as the paper.

2. Color fish with markers using a variety of dots, strokes, and dashes, leaving some white spaces. Do not color the background.

3. Using paintbrushes and water, blend colors of markers to get lighter hues, additional colors, and so on to fill in white spaces in fish.

4. Paint light blue watercolor around the fish.

5. Outline the fish with a black marker.

6. Seaweeds may be added with a green marker.

Design Element: Area—hard and soft edges; Space—overlap
Art History: J. M. W. Turner for hard and soft edges
Grade Level: Lower primary

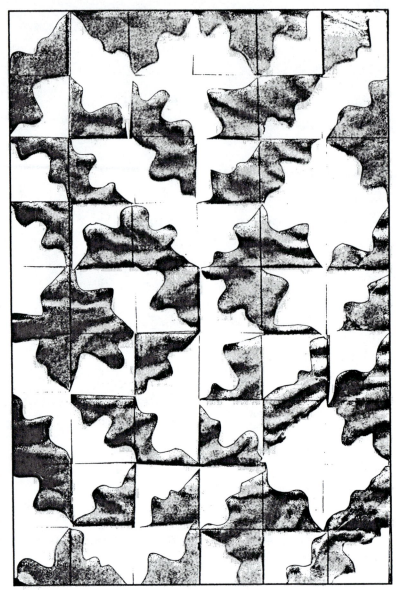

...onstruction

...-by-3-inch
...paper, all one
color
- glue
- scissors
- ruler
- pencil

Directions

Have students:

1. On any color of 12-by-18-inch construction paper, mark off a grid of 3-by-3-inch squares.

2. Choose one color of 3-by-3-inch squares. You will need 12 squares.

3. Draw one type of line from one corner diagonally to another corner. Some suggestions are shown below.

4. Cut out and glue both pieces somewhere on the grid system, but not side by side.

5. On the next 3-by-3-inch piece of paper, draw the same type of line but vary it somehow. Try not to make it exactly like the first one. Cut and glue down, but do not glue the two pieces side by side.

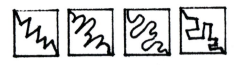

6. Continue with variations of your line until the paper is filled.

Design Element: Area—positive and negative shapes;
Line—creating shape; Composition—repetition with unity and variety.

Art History: Matisse for positive and negative shapes

Grade Level: Intermediate

Materials

- 12-by-18-inch tagboard
- tempera paint
- pencil

- paintbrush
- ruler

Directions

Have students:

1. On tagboard, draw the following "landscape lines": prairie, hogback, foothills, 10,000-foot mountains, and 14,000-foot mountains.

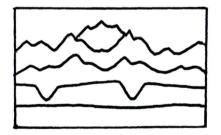

2. Use a ruler to draw horizontal lines that are different distances apart over the landscape lines.

3. In each space between the lines, draw three angle lines.

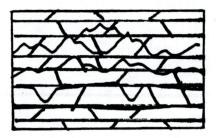

4. Using the different mixtures of the colors listed below, paint the different shapes in the prairie, each mountain range, and the sky.

sky	blue + white
14,000 ft. mountain	blue + white + orange
10,000 ft. mountain	blue + white + violet
foothills	blue + green + white
hogback	blue + green
prairie	green + yellow

Example: for the sky, paint the shapes with varying mixtures of blue and white. Try to mix as many different hues as possible.

Design Element: Area—color shapes; Color—hues and color showing depth

Art History: Paul Cézanne's *Mont Sainte-Victoire* for color shapes

Grade Level: Intermediate

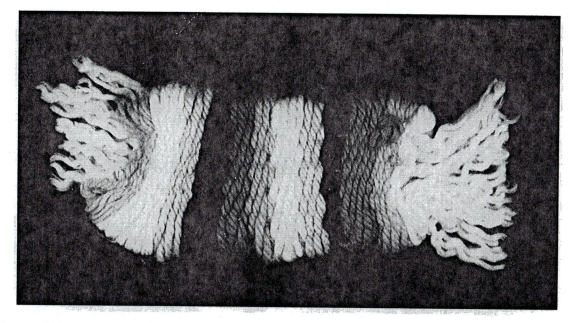

Materials

- 6-by-9-inch practice paper
- 6-by-9-inch cardboard
- scissors
- string
- various colors of yarn

- visual references of Native American weavings, especially the patterns and symbols
- pencil

Directions

Have students:

1. On 6-by-9-inch practice paper, choose a Native American symbol to draw. Make it large, but not so large that it touches the edges.

2. Shade the back of the practice paper (this works the same as carbon paper) to transfer it to 6-by-9-inch cardboard.

3. On 6-by-9-inch cardboard, mark off every ½ inch on two opposite sides and cut in on those marks ½ inch.

4. To create warp, start at one corner cut with white string and go across to the opposite cut, then to its neighboring cut, then back across to the opposite cut. Continue until the string is in the last cut. The strings should go across the front of the design and not the back.

5. Use color yarn to weave into the design first. Tie onto white string, then weave over, under, over, under. Tie string when you get to the end of the string or the design. If weaving a line pattern, start at the top.

6. To weave the background, use the same process but remember to weave around the last string of the design (if not, a hole will remain).

7. Slip weaving off cardboard and tie tassels onto the loops where the white string used to be hooked on the cardboard.

Design Element: Area—color shapes

Art History: Navajo weavings for color shapes

Grade Level: Intermediate

Exploding Shapes

Materials

- 6-by-9-inch construction paper
- scissors
- glue
- 12-by-18-inch construction paper
- envelope
- pencil

Directions

Have students:

1. On a sheet of 6-by-9-inch construction paper, draw *V*'s, *W*'s, or *U*'s that go off the edge but do not touch in the middle. Draw at least five.

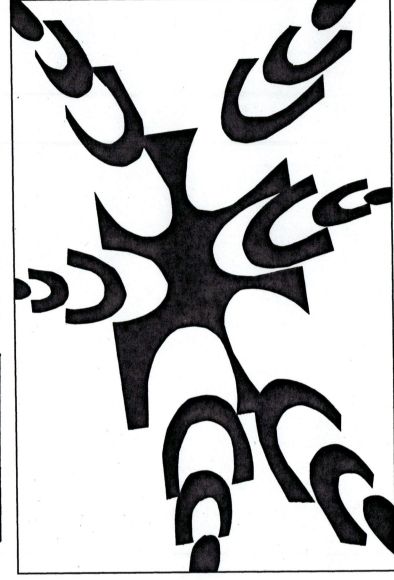

2. Draw the chosen "letter" inside the first shape until the shape is filled. Letters should be ½ inch apart.

3. Cut out the shapes that were drawn in step 1, but do not cut the shapes drawn in step 2. Place shapes in an envelope.

5. Glue down center shape first onto a 12-by-18-inch piece of construction paper.

6. Select one of the shapes and cut out the shapes drawn in step 2 one at a time. Glue down the shapes in order, but glued a little further apart each time.

7. Repeat with the remaining shapes. The last piece from each shape should touch the edge of the 12-by-18-inch paper.

Design Element: Area—shapes within shapes

Art History: Matisse for paper cut-outs

Grade Level: Intermediate

Materials
- real or artificial plant for visual reference
- 12-by-18-inch practice paper
- 12-by-18-inch yellow construction paper
- newspaper
- color chalk
- pencil

Directions
Have students:

1. On 12-by-18-inch practice paper, draw a part of the plant. Do not draw the entire plant.

2. At a window, light source (i.e., light table), or with carbon paper, transfer onto yellow construction paper.

3. Color background with blue and dark green shapes. Blend together with fingers.

4. Color leaves with yellow-green chalk. Do not blend.

5. Color veins with green chalk and blend with fingertip once.

6. For highlights and shadows, use white chalk for the top of leaves and brown for the bottom of leaves. Do not blend. Always use newspaper to work on and in which to store your work.

Design Element: Area—hard and soft edges; Value—highlight and shadow; Space—*distinct* versus *diminished* detail

Art History: Rembrandt Van Rijn for hard and soft edges, highlight and shadow

Grade Level: Intermediate

Materials

- 12-by-18-inch practice paper
- 12-by-18-inch white drawing paper
- markers or paints
- pencil

Directions

Have students:

1. On 12-by-18-inch practice paper, draw a section or part of a tree that has lost its leaves.

2. Draw the negative areas or the empty spots where you can see the sky. Make sure the branches touch the edge of your paper.

3. At a window, light source (i.e., light table), or with carbon paper, transfer onto 12-by-18-inch white paper.

4. Choose three analogous colors of markers or paints, that is, colors that are neighbors on the color wheel.

5. Color or paint the areas that go off the top edge of the paper the first analogous color and color or paint the shapes or areas that go off the bottom edge the third analogous color.

6. Color the shapes in between the second analogous color, or the mixture of the first and third colors.

7. Paint tree branches black.

Design Element: Area—negative area; Color—analogous colors

Art History: Mondrian for negative areas of color

Grade Level: Intermediate

Materials

- 12-by-18-inch practice paper
- 12-by-18-inch white construction paper
- carbon paper
- markers
- ruler
- pencil

Directions

Have students:

1. On 12-by-18-inch practice paper, sketch a front door and porch.

2. At a window, light source (i.e., light table), or with carbon paper, transfer the image to the 12-by-18-inch white construction paper.

3. Draw two vertical lines and three horizontal lines across the drawing. Lines should not be parallel.

4. With a marker, color the shapes in a positive-negative manner and reverse in each section. For example, if the wall is black in one section, the wall should be white in the next one.

Design Element: Area—positive and negative shapes

Art History: Marc Chagall's *I and the Village* for positive and negative shapes

Grade Level: Upper elementary

Linoleum Bicycle Print

Materials

- practice drawing from "Negative Area Bicycle" (see p. 104) reduced to 6 by 9 inches
- 6-by-9-inch linoleum
- carbon paper
- brayer
- printer's ink
- 6-by-9-inch plexiglass sheet
- 9-by-24-inch white construction paper
- linoleum carving tools*
- pencil

Directions

Have students:

1. Once students have finished the "Negative Area Bicycle" project, reduce it 50 percent by hand or on photocopier.

2. Use carbon paper to transfer it to linoleum.

3. Carve out the bike. Remember to cut away from the hand.

4. Squirt a dime-size pile of printer's ink onto plexiglass.

5. Roll out the ink using the brayer.

6. With the ink on the brayer, roll the brayer over the linoleum.

7. Take one of the four 9-by-24-inch white sheets of paper and place on linoleum, press gently to transfer ink, print with one analogous color four times. (Once for each sheet.) For example, let's say blue.

*Review with students safety precautions in using knives. Cut away from your hand. Do not walk around with the knife. Have cardboard underneath. Do not talk while cutting. Knives are not toys.

8. Next, carve out the areas to be kept blue.

9. Print the next color (as in steps 4--7), for example, green four times, on top of blue.

10. Carve out areas to be kept green.

11. Print the third color (as in steps 4--7) four times on top of green.

12. Ask students to choose the best print or prints to hand in.

Design Element: Area—negative area, scale and proportion

Art History: Japanese wood-block prints for color shapes

Grade Level: Upper elementary

Georgia O'Keeffe Flower

Materials

- 12-by-18-inch practice paper
- 12-by-18-inch tagboard
- assortment of artificial flowers for visual reference
- assorted colors of tissue paper
- polymer gloss medium
- paintbrush
- paint tray
- black permanent markers
- X-ACTO knife*
- pencil

Directions

Have students:

1. On 12-by-18-inch practice paper, draw a close-up of one of the plastic flowers. Make the drawing appear as if you are looking into the flower. Make the flower touch all four edges of the paper.

2. Plan out where four colors of tissue will go.

3. Transfer to tagboard by shading the back of the paper with pencil to create your own carbon paper.

4. Pour a small amount of polymer into one compartment of a paint tray.

5. Brush polymer on one shape, lay tissue down and then cut on the outside edge of the shape with an X-ACTO knife. If you cut where the polymer has been placed, the tissue will rip. Do not brush polymer over the top of the tissue.

6. Continue attaching tissue until the whole surface is covered.

7. Once all the tissue has been attached, brush polymer over the entire surface.

8. Outline shape with black permanent marker.

Design Element: Area—simplified shapes; Composition—open composition

Art History: Georgia O'Keeffe for simplified shapes

Grade Level: Upper elementary

*Review with students safety precautions in using knives. Cut away from your hand. Do not walk around with the knife. Have cardboard underneath. Do not talk while cutting. Knives are not toys.

Georgia O'Keeffe Batik

Materials

- 12-by-18-inch paper
- 12-by-18-inch piece of unbleached muslin
- batik wax
- electric skillet
- batik paintbrush
- watercolor paintbrush
- push pins
- frame
- batik dye
- paper towels
- plastic flowers for visual reference
- iron
- newspapers
- pencil

Directions

Have students:

1. On 12-by-18-inch practice paper, draw a contour study of a flower. Outline the shape of the petals and color shapes. Look into the flower from the top, not the side. Your drawing should look like a "paint-by-number picture" before it is painted. Your drawing should touch the edge of the paper.

2. At a window, light source (i.e., light table), or with carbon paper, transfer onto cloth using a pencil.

3. With batik dye, brush in the colors in the various shapes. Use water to blend.

4. Once dry, pin cloth to frame and wax the shapes you want to keep colored. Make sure the wax goes through to the back side. If it did not, wax on the back.

5. Once waxed, dip in black batik dye. Wipe off dye bubbles on waxed areas.

6. Let dry. Wax black areas.

7. Iron out wax by placing waxed cloth between newspaper.

Design Element: Area—color shapes

Art History: O'Keeffe for color shapes

Grade Level: Upper elementary

Materials

- bicycle for visual reference
- 12-by-18-inch manila paper
- 12-by-18-inch white drawing paper
- felt-tip pens
- markers
- pencil

Directions

Have students:

1. On 12-by-18-inch manila paper, draw either the front half or the back half of the bicycle by drawing the negative areas. Concentrate on edges. Do not draw any lines in the positive area, that is, the actual bike.

2. Be sure all parts are in proportion. Double check your lines and shapes by sighting them up with your pencil.

3. At a window, light source (i.e., light table), or with carbon paper, transfer onto 12-by-18-inch white drawing paper.

4. With felt-tip pens, fill each negative area shape with a different type of line. Have consistent line patterns in each shape.

5. With marker, color bicycle in a solid color.

Design Element: Area—negative shapes; Line—line variety

Art History: Mondrian's early tree paintings for negative shapes

Grade Level: Upper elementary

Materials

- 9-by-12-inch practice paper
- 2 sheets of 9-by-12-inch poster board
- 9-by-12-inch white construction paper
- water-based printer's ink
- brayers (2)
- plexiglass sheet or formica top
- printing press or may substitute with brayers
- scissors
- carbon paper
- visual references of Eskimo animal art
- glue
- pencil

Directions

Have students:

1. On 9-by-12-inch practice paper, draw a sketch of an animal that Eskimos would hunt. Students may design their own from visual references or by using the simplified shapes used by the Eskimos to draw animals.

2. Plan out what shapes will be used to show the animal. (These shapes will be cut out and glued onto a piece of poster board.)

3. Transfer shapes onto poster board using carbon paper.

4. Trace outline of animal onto a second piece of poster board using carbon paper.

5. Cut out shapes from posterboard in step 3 and glue onto second piece of poster board. Make sure shapes are close together.

6. Once the animal is finished, design a border made of two types of Eskimo border motifs. Cut from posterboard scraps, and glue at the top or bottom of the 9-by-12-inch posterboard. The two border motifs should be repeated on two edges.

7. Cut out backgrounds.

8. Squirt a dime-size pile of printer's ink onto plexiglass.

9. Roll out the ink using the brayer.

10. With the ink on the brayer, roll the brayer over the cardboard.

11. Place 9-by-12-inch white construction paper on top of inked cardboard.

12. Run through press or by rolling over it with a clean brayer to make a print.

Design Element: Area—simplified shapes

Art History: Eskimo art for simplified shapes

Grade Level: Upper elementary

Toucan Reduction Print

Materials

- 6-by-9-inch practice paper
- visual references of toucans
- water-based markers
- 6-by-9-inch white construction paper
- 6-by-9-inch Styrofoam
- 9-by-12-inch watercolor paper

- scissors
- brown tempera paint
- masking tape
- paintbrush
- pencil
- carbon paper

Directions

Have students:

1. On 6-by-9-inch practice paper, draw a toucan as large as possible.

2. Color or mark in the color shapes.

3. Trace outside shape of the toucan onto Styrofoam using carbon paper.

4. With markers, color in one shape, for example, blue.

5. Place Styrofoam on white paper to make a print. If the marker dries on the Styrofoam, lightly moisten the white paper before printing.

6. Cut out blue shape from Styrofoam or press down with pencil.

7. Print the next color, let's say green.

8. Cut out green shapes from Styrofoam or press down with pencil.

9. Color all remaining parts the third color, let's say yellow.

10. Cut out or press down yellow parts of Styrofoam.

11. Print fourth color, let's say orange.

12. Cut out or press down orange.

13. Print fifth color, let's say red.

14. Outline feathers, eyes, beak with fine point black felt-tip pen. Cut out toucan.

15. Tape watercolor paper to table.

16. Wet whole paper and with watercolor paints; paint green, yellow, and blue shapes. The colors should bleed together.

17. Once the watercolor paper is dry, glue on toucan.

18. With brown tempera, paint a branch with three smaller branches.

19. With watercolor, paint three yellow-green leaves with dark green veins on each branch. Outline with black felt-tip pen.

Design Element: Area—color shapes

Art History: Japanese prints for color shapes

Grade Level: Upper elementary

Picasso Still Life

Materials

- still-life objects
- 12-by-18-inch practice paper
- 12-by-18-inch tagboard
- tissue paper
- polymer gloss medium
- paintbrush
- black felt-tip marker (permanent)
- pencil

Directions

Have students:

1. On 12-by-18-inch practice paper, draw the still life, looking for letter shapes and geometric shapes that make up the objects. Look at proportions, that is, how the parts of the objects line up.

2. At a window, light source (i.e., light table), or with carbon paper, transfer onto tagboard with pencil.

3. Choose three to five colors of tissue paper.

4. Without drawing on the tissue, tear out the shapes of the objects by just looking at the objects.

5. Attach to tagboard with polymer gloss medium. Clean brushes with hot water.

6. When the polymer is dry, outline the original drawn shapes with black felt-tip marker.

Design Element: Area—proportion and scale, hard versus soft edges.

Art History: Picasso's Rose Period for color shapes

Grade Level: Upper elementary

Materials

- 12-by-18-inch practice paper
- 12-by-18-inch tagboard or watercolor paper
- bicycle picture for visual reference
- Caran D'Ache or water-soluble crayons
- paintbrush
- pencil

Directions

Have students:

1. On 12-by-18-inch practice paper, draw half of the bicycle. Be sure to draw the negative areas and have the bicycle touch all four edges of the paper.

2. At a window, light source (i.e., light table), or with carbon paper, transfer onto tagboard or watercolor paper.

3. Choose three analogous colors of Caran D'Ache to outline the negative areas, including the sides of the paper.

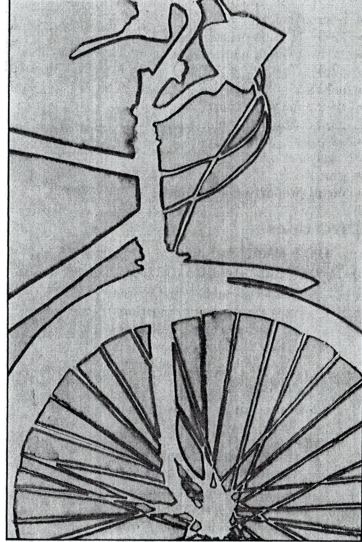

4. Use a small brush and water to "pull" the Caran D'Ache into the negative areas. The bicycle should remain white.

Design Element: Area—negative area

Art History: Mondrian trees for negative areas

Grade Level: Upper elementary

Materials

- mirror
- 12-by-18-inch practice paper
- 12-by-18-inch white drawing paper
- pencil
- tissue for use as tortillons or paper stumps for blending
- scissors
- construction paper
- glue
- facial proportion guidelines

Directions

Have students:

1 Using a facial proportion guideline and a mirror, see how your facial proportions compare to the guidelines. Have students draw their faces on 12-by-18-inch practice paper.

2. Trace onto 12-by-18-inch white drawing paper.

3. Draw in shadows with rolled tissue or a paper stump. (Apply pencil lead on a piece of paper, rub corner or point of tissue or paper stump over the pencil lead and then gently rub tissue point or pointed corner of paper stump areas of face where shadows are desired.)

4. Shade in hair, eyes, lips, eyebrows, and so on.

5. Cut out portrait and glue on construction paper.

6. Have students save their practice drawings for ceramic self-portraits (see page 193).

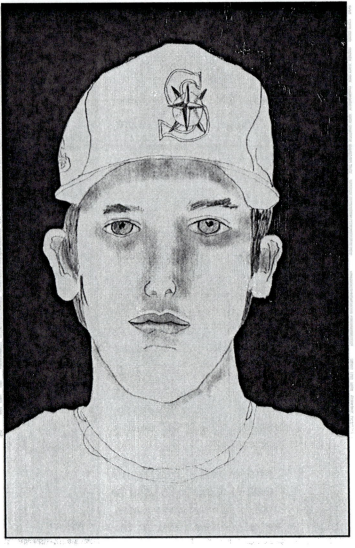

Design Element: Area—proportion, scale; Value—highlights and shadows

Art History: Alex Katz for value shapes

Grade Level: Upper elementary

Chapter

4
Texture

The study of the design element of **texture** challenges the student to represent the "feel" of an object's surface. For a student to understand this element, he needs to discover what repeating lines and shapes make up a given texture. For example, the student might represent the texture of sand using repeating dots. To show the texture of wood grain, the student might use concentric circles. For feathers, the student might use thin parallel lines. The study of any texture requires the student to realize that all textures have some kind of repeating patterns in their lines and shapes. Once again, the student needs to look at an object in a different manner—what is seen, not the student's perception of what he thinks he sees.

Types of Texture

At the elementary level, the study of texture may incorporate different types of textures studies that represent how various objects feel. For example, a piece of art may contain actual texture, or **encaustic texture**. One way to create an encaustic texture is to apply a thick layer of acrylic paint. Mixing liquid starch with tempera provides a cheaper alternative to acrylic paint, which can be expensive. Crayons can be melted in muffin tins on a bread warmer and applied to paper with cotton swabs to create an encaustic surface texture. Encaustic texture can be found in Vincent Van Gogh's *Starry Night*. He applied thick brushstrokes of oil paint to create sky, trees, mountains, and buildings. The painting has actual texture. The student should understand that the texture of the paint need not represent how the object actually feels. A sky does not have lumpy, linear texture. Therefore, encaustic texture may or may not be considered representational.

Collage

Another form of encaustic texture is found in **collage**. A **collage** is made of any material or item that can be attached to a surface. Whether using yarn, beans, rice, or pieces of wood, the student will need to consider the **principles of organization** to achieve a balanced composition. *Le Courier* by Georges Braque is an example of collage that grew out of the Cubism movement of the early 1900s.

Papier-Collé

Papier-collé, a variation of collage, incorporates the use of torn or cut paper to decorate a picture plane. The student may use such items as construction paper, newspaper, magazine pictures, wallpaper, and tissue paper to represent the subject matter. Henri Matisse used cut paper to create the simplified shapes in *The Beasts of the Sea*.

Texture for Decoration

Texture may be used simply for **decoration** of a surface. The texture is not meant to represent an object but it is enjoyed for its lines and patterns. This decorative texture may also be referred to as **invented texture**. At the elementary level, texture rubbings with crayons provide an excellent means of decorating a picture plane. Every object has some type of texture, and anything can be used to make a texture rubbing. *The Kiss* by Gustav Klimt shows a richly decorated surface where the human figures appear secondary.

Texture and Emotion

Emotions and *moods* can be relayed by texture. Whether one wants to portray the power of a king, the sadness of old age, or the inherent beauty in nature, texture studies offer many possibilities for expressing emotions and moods. For the elementary level, an interesting project involves drawing a still life of various kinds of fruit and decorating the objects with textures that do not represent the objects. For example, an apple with very rough texture would not be very appetizing. Ivan Albright's *And God Created Man in His Own Image* shows how exaggerated texture can produce an emotional effect.

Texture and Space

Space can be shown through the use of texture. Bold and detailed texture appears closer to the viewer than fuzzy and small texture lines and shapes, which appear to be in the distance. Albert Bierstadt's landscape paintings, including *The Rocky Mountains*, incorporate detailed textural representation on the objects in the foreground. As one's eye travels to the objects in the distance, the objects become less detailed and fuzzy in appearance, creating the illusion of depth and distance.

Descriptive Texture

One of the most challenging aspects in the study of texture involves the descriptive use of texture. *Descriptive texture*, also referred to as *simulated texture* or *objective texture*, requires the student to represent how an object feels through careful study and rendering of the lines and shapes that make up the textural surfaces of the object. The student must be able to discern what lines or shapes make up a textural surface and have fine motor skills to draw or paint the texture. Consequently, the study of descriptive texture works well at the middle school or high school level. The art of Photo-realists Chuck Close and Richard Estes shows a very realistic, objective study and rendering of textural surfaces.

Materials

- three handouts—one that has a three-inch diameter circle, a three-inch equilateral triangle, and a 3-by-3-inch square (each handout should have a circle, triangle and a square)
- crayons
- oil pastels
- 12-by-18-inch construction paper
- glue
- scissors
- various textured objects for rubbings (i.e., sandpaper [various levels of rough], woods, leaves, cardboard, coins, bubble packing, etc.)

Directions

Have students:

1. Choose any three analogous colors of crayons.

2. On the three handouts, make texture rubbings using crayons. Use a different color for each sheet.

3. Carefully cut out the circle, triangle, and square. With lower primary students, stress cutting on the line.

4. Arrange the nine shapes on a sheet of 12-by-18-inch construction paper that is one of the analogous colors (so that the entire picture plane is balanced). Colors and shapes should balance each other (e.g., do not place all the circles on one side of the paper).

5. Glue down the shapes on the construction paper by placing small dabs of glue on the back of the shapes' edges.

6. Using the same analogous colors of oil pastel, draw contour lines around the shapes until all the negative area is filled.

Design Element: Texture—decorative; Line—contour lines;
Color—analogous colors

Art History: Picasso's Constructivism Period for decorative texture

Grade Level: Lower primary

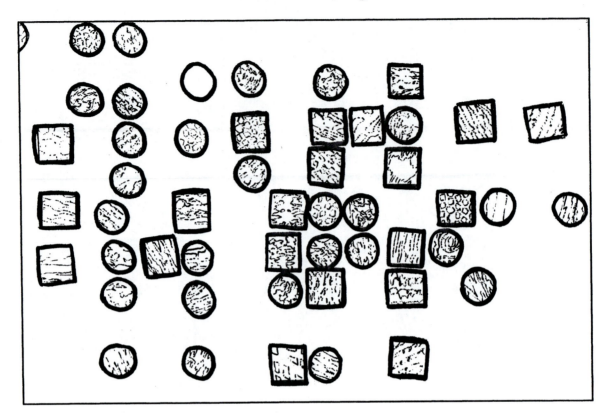

Materials

- handout with 25 one-inch diameter circles
- handout with 20 one-by-one-inch squares
- 12-by-18-inch construction paper
- crayons

- various textured objects for rubbings (i.e., sandpaper [various levels of rough], woods, leaves, cardboard, coins, bubble packing, etc.)
- scissors
- glue

Directions

Have students:

1. Choose three analogous colors of crayon.

2. Make a texture rubbing in each circle and square. Find as many different textures as you can.

3. Cut out the circles and squares.

4. On 12-by-18-inch construction paper, arrange circles and squares in rows vertically and horizontally to use the entire picture plane. You may skip spaces in the vertical and horizontal rows, but when the shapes are side by side, keep a pencil width between them.

5. Glue the shapes onto construction paper.

Design Element: Texture—decoration

Art History: Picasso for decorative texture

Grade Level: Lower primary

Materials

- four handouts that have various sizes of squares and rectangles
- crayons
- various textured objects for rubbings (i.e., sandpaper [various levels of rough], woods, leaves, cardboard, coins, bubble packing, etc.)
- 12-by-18-inch construction paper
- glue
- scissors

Directions

Have students:

1. Choose three analogous colors of crayon.

2. On three handouts, use crayons to make texture rubbings in the square and rectangular shapes. Use one color per handout.

3. On the fourth handout, use all three colors and repeat textures if desired.

4. Carefully cut out the shapes.

5. On 12-by-18-inch construction paper that is one of the analogous colors or black, start in one corner and arrange the shapes like bricks so that there is one pencil width between each "brick." Try not to have the same color side by side.

6. Glue down remaining shapes in the same manner.

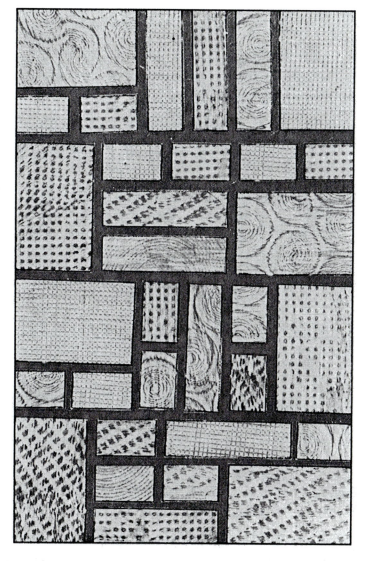

Design Element: Texture—decoration

Art History: Picasso for decorative texture

Grade Level: Lower primary

Materials

- 12-by-18-inch practice paper
- 12-by-18-inch thin white paper (or 8-by-11-inch photocopy paper)
- 12-by-18-inch construction paper
- visual references of cowboy boot designs
- crayons
- black felt-tip pen
- pencil
- various textured objects for rubbings (i.e., sandpaper [various levels of rough], woods, leaves, cardboard, coins, bubble packing, etc.)
- scissors
- glue

Directions

Have students:

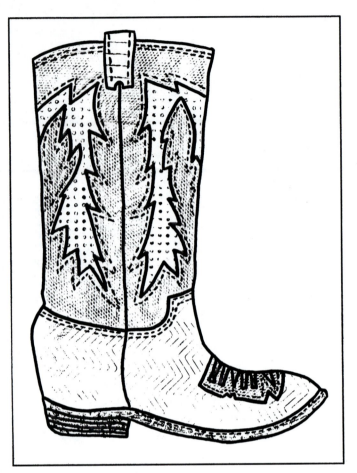

1. On 12-by-18-inch practice paper, draw a side view of a cowboy boot.

2. Draw a line down the center of the boot so it is divided in half.

3. Draw a design on one side.

4. Fold the paper in half along the center line of the boot and trace the design onto the other side to make a symmetrical design.

5. Trace the design onto 12-by-18-inch white paper.

6. Make texture rubbings in your designs with crayon.

7. With a black felt-tip pen, outline your designs and draw stitch marks (see fig. above).

8. Cut out the boot and glue on any color of construction paper.

Design Element: Texture—decoration; Composition—symmetry

Art History: Ivan Albright for decorative texture

Grade Level: Intermediate

Materials

- students' tennis shoes for visual reference
- crayons
- 12-by-18-inch practice paper
- 12-by-18-inch white drawing paper
- markers
- pencil

Directions

Have students:

1. On 12-by-18-inch practice paper, draw the outline of three different shoes (one of each). Make them overlap and also touch each edge of the paper.

2. Choose three analogous colors of crayon and mark where they will be used on the paper. The same color may touch at corners of shapes created by the overlapping of the shoes but not on the sides of the shapes created by the overlapping of the shoes.

3. At a window, light source (i.e., light table), or with carbon paper, transfer the shapes onto 12-by-18-inch white drawing paper.

4. Using crayon, fill in the shapes with texture rubbings from the bottoms of shoes.

5. With one of the analogous colors, outline the shapes with marker.

Design Element: Texture—decorative;
Composition—asymmetrical balance

Art History: Georges Braque for decorative texture

Grade Level: Intermediate

Materials

- 2 sheets 12-by-18-inch practice paper
- objects for tabletop still life
- 12-by-18-inch tagboard
- wallpaper (assorted patterns and colors)
- carbon paper
- scissors
- glue
- pencil
- permanent markers

Directions

Have students:

1. Draw still life arranged on a table onto 12-by-18-inch practice paper, showing silhouette of objects.

2. Trace the lines with a black marker.

3. Make a second copy of the drawing by using a window, light source (i.e., light table), or carbon paper to transfer the still life onto another sheet of paper (one sheet will be cut up for pattern pieces).

4. Cut and glue two wallpaper patterns onto 12-by-18-inch tagboard to show a tabletop and background. Patterns should contrast.

5. Using one of the still-life pictures, cut out the shapes and trace (using carbon paper) onto wallpaper. Patterns should contrast.

6. Cut out the wallpaper shapes.

7. Glue the shapes onto tagboard, referring to the intact still-life picture for placement.

8. Outline the shapes with permanent marker.

Design Element: Texture—collage

Art History: Braque for an example of collage

Grade Level: Intermediate

Mountain Range Texture

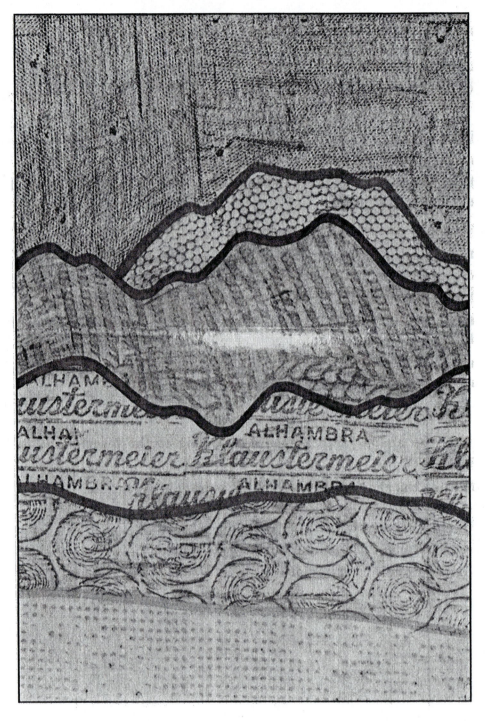

Materials

- 18-by-24-inch white drawing paper
- crayons
- markers
- various textured objects for rubbings (i.e., sandpaper [various levels of rough], woods, leaves, cardboard, coins, bubble packing, etc.)
- pencil

Directions

Have students:

1. On 18-by-24-inch white paper, draw (starting at the bottom of the paper and moving up, leaving space at the top of the picture for the sky):

   a. plains
   b. foothills
   c. first range of mountains
   d. a second range of mountains taller than the first range
   e. a third range of mountains taller than the second range

2. With crayon, make a texture rubbing on the plains with a warm color (yellow, orange, or red) and a bold texture.

3. Make texture rubbings, moving up the paper: each successive mountain range should have a finer texture and the next color on a color wheel with primary, secondary, and tertiary colors. The sky will have the smoothest texture and should be a cool color (blue-violet or violet).

4. Outline each mountain range with a marker that is the same color as the texture rubbings in that range.

Design Element: Texture—showing space through sharp versus diminished detail

Art History: Jacob van Ruisdael for textures showing depth

Grade Level: Intermediate

Textured Flower

Materials

- 12-by-18-inch practice paper
- 12-by-18-inch thin white paper
- artificial flowers for visual reference
- ruler
- crayons
- markers
- pencil
- various textured objects for rubbings (i.e., sandpaper [various levels of rough], woods, leaves, cardboard, coins, bubble packing, etc.)

Directions

Have students:

1. On 12-by-18-inch practice paper, draw a flower, stem, and leaves that touch all four edges of the paper.

2. Trace the design onto a sheet of thin 12-by-18-inch paper.

3. Use a ruler to draw four vertical lines that are not parallel and seven horizontal lines that are not parallel.

4. With crayon, make a texture rubbing in each shape. Use one color for the flower, but make a different texture rubbing for each shape. Do the same for the stem, leaves, and background but with a different color for each.

5. Use markers that are the same colors as the crayon to trace over your horizontal and vertical lines. The lines will change colors as they go through the background, flower, stem, and leaves. Outline the flower, leaves, and stem using markers that are the same colors as the crayon.

Design Element: Texture—decoration

Art History: Dubuffet for decorative texture

Grade Level: Upper elementary

Materials

- handout with 24 2-by-2-inch squares
- 12-by-18-inch thin white paper
- various textured objects for rubbings (i.e., sandpaper [various levels of rough], woods, leaves, cardboard, coins, bubble packing, etc.)
- color chalk
- crayons (black and white)
- pencil

Directions

Have students:

1. Using a black crayon, make texture rubbings on the handout.

2. Fold a sheet of thin 12-by-18-inch white paper in half to 9 by 12 inches.

3. With the paper folded so the fold is to the left, use a pencil to draw patio stone shapes on the top surface. Leave ¼-inch gap between all shapes.

4. Using a pencil fill in each shape with a drawn texture using the texture rubbings as a reference.

5. Open the folded paper and on the right side, color blotches of colored chalk.

6. Color over the chalk with white crayon.

7. Using black crayon, color over the white crayon.

8. Fold the paper along the original fold and color in texture patterns with pencil. Press hard to get a good transfer.

9. Open folded paper for finished project.

Design Element: Texture—decoration

Art History: Ivan Albright for decorative texture

Grade Level: Upper elementary

Materials

- handout with 24 2-by-2-inch squares for making texture rubbings
- black crayon
- various textured objects for rubbings (i.e., sandpaper [various levels of rough], woods, leaves, cardboard, coins, bubble packing, etc.)
- 9-by-12-inch white paper
- 9-by-12-inch muslin pieces
- batik wax (paraffin, beeswax)
- batik dye
- clothespins
- iron
- electric skillet for melting wax
- newspaper
- wooden stick or small dowels that are sharpened
- stapler
- pencil
- paper towels

Directions

Have students:

1. Using a black crayon, make 24 different texture rubbings on the handout.

2. On 9-by-12-inch white paper, draw three unparallel lines on the short side and four unparallel lines on the long side to create 20 shapes.

3. Draw textures in the shapes, using the handout as a reference.

4. Melt the batik wax in a skillet. Dip the muslin into the skillet of wax (use clothespins to hold the top corners while dipping).

5. Staple the 9-by-12-inch paper, design side up, on the back of the waxed cloth.

6. With a wooden stick or small sharpened dowel, scratch the lines and shapes of the textures into the waxed cloth.

7. After removing the stapled paper, brush one or several colors of batik dye onto the muslin. Wipe off excess dye.

8. Place cloth between several layers of newspaper. Iron out wax. (The wax will melt into the newspaper.)

Design Element: Texture—decoration

Art History: Batiks from Java or Africa

Grade Level: Upper elementary

Chapter

5

Value

By definition, the study of *value* involves showing how light wraps around an object. The student must understand that the various shapes of highlights and shadows on an object create the sense of volume. (The concept of color values is addressed in chapter 6, "Color.") This can be a difficult concept for the lower primary student; however, the student may be given exposure to the concept of value through projects that incorporate the *decorative* use of value and the *achromatic* aspect of value. A decorative use of color is a balanced arrangement of the achromatic values, blacks through grays to white, in a composition that can be objective, subjective, or non-objective. By focusing on the achromatic aspect of value– that is, using strictly blacks, grays, and whites– the student may also gain development of the fine motor skills necessary for controlling various mediums to show various values. For example, a project may use black, gray, and white oil pastels or crayons in a design of various sizes of squares and rectangles, as in a Piet Mondrian's *Composition with Red, Blue, and Yellow*, simply to afford the student practice in blending a consistent even value without streaks and creating a balanced composition with the three values.

Value and Space

To create the illusion of *space* (volume), the student must be able to see the shapes, whether *geometric* or *biomorphic*, of the following four values on a surface: the whitest area is called the *highlight*; the lightest gray, *light*; medium gray, *penumbra*; and the darkest area, *umbra*. Focusing strictly on the shapes of these values, the student will be able to make a simple circle appear as a sphere, for example. The values can be more easily seen and identified when the subject matter is illuminated by a single light source (window light, a spotlight, etc.). A *multiple light* source, light that covers an object from all angles, tends to flatten an object because the values become uniform. The *single light* source in Caravaggio's *The Calling of St. Matthew* creates a sense of depth and volume while the multiple light source in Edouard Manet's *The Fifer* tends to flatten the figure by reducing the number of values shown on the surface of the figure and eliminating shadows.

Value and Emotion

Value may be used to portray *emotion*, drama, and character through the use of *high contrast* and *low contrast*. High contrast incorporates the use of black and white with few grays while low contrast uses mostly grays and little black and white. One example of high contrast can be found in the use of *chiaroscuro*, figures coming in and out of shadows, as in Rembrandt's *The Night Watch*. His treatment of value creates mystery and drama. An extreme version of chiaroscuro, called *tenebrism*, shows parts of figures hidden in shadows, thereby creating a very dramatic setting, as seen in Georges de la Tour's *Joseph the Carpenter*. An example of the use of high contrast can be found in Edvard Munch's *The Scream*. The figure and lines are black and white, adding to the emotional effect of the scene. An example of the use of low contrast can be found in the work of Sandro Botticelli, in particular *The Birth of Venus*. The lack of black and white adds to the sense of calmness and serenity.

Materials

- 12-by-18-inch white construction paper
- 1-by-12-inch black construction paper strips
- scissors
- pencil

Directions

Have students:

1. Fold a sheet of 12-by-18-inch white construction paper in half to 9 by 12 inches.

2. Draw a line one inch from the outer edge (not at the fold).

3. Draw "op" lines from the folded edge to the line drawn in step 2. Each "op-line" design has lines that vary in distance from each other. Some possibilities are shown below.

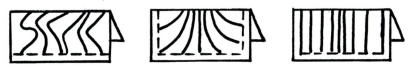

4. While paper is folded, cut your "op" lines. Do not cut past the line drawn in step 2.

5. Unfold white paper and weave 1-by-12-inch black strips into place. Strips should be tightly woven.

Design Element: Value—high contrast; Area—creating optical movement

Art History: Op Art; Bridget Riley for high contrast

Grade Level: Intermediate

Materials

- photograph of the student
- opaque projector
- 9-by-12-inch graph paper with ¼-inch squares
- pencil
- scissors
- colored markers
- 12-by-18-inch construction paper

Directions

Have students:

1. Help students use opaque projector to trace photograph onto 12-by-8-inch graph paper with ¼-inch squares. With pencil, outline light, medium, and dark areas.

2. Using light, medium, and dark colors of marker, color in each square. If a line passes through a square, the square must be one of the colors.

3. Cut out portrait and mount on construction paper.

Design Element: Value—value shapes

Art History: Picasso's and Braque's Cubism Periods for value shapes

Grade Level: Intermediate

Materials

- still-life objects
- 12-by-18-inch practice paper
- 12-by-18-inch white construction paper
- 12-by-18-inch construction paper (any color, but white)
- black felt-tip pen
- pencil
- ruler
- scissors

Directions

Have students:

1. On 12-by-18-inch practice paper, draw the outside contour line of any four still-life objects in the classroom. Draw the objects to show transparent overlap (see figure).

2. At a window, light source (i.e., light table), or with carbon paper, transfer the design to 12-by-18-inch white construction paper.

3. In one object, draw vertical lines close together with a black felt-tip pen.

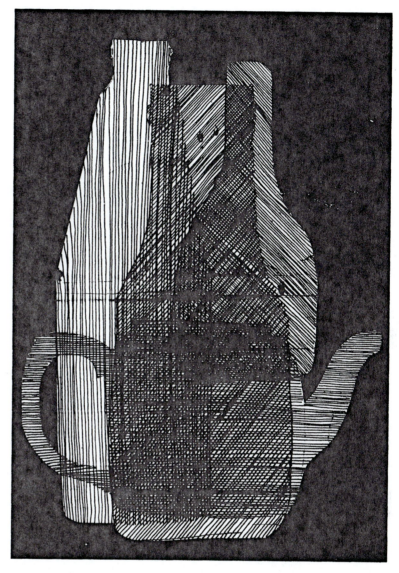

4. In a second object, draw horizontal lines.

5. In a third object, draw 45-degree lines angling down to the right.

6. In the fourth object, draw 45-degree lines angling down to the left.

7. Cut out still life and glue on any color of 12-by-18-inch construction paper.

Design Element: Value—crosshatch lines showing value

Art History: Dürer for crosshatch lines

Grade Level: Intermediate

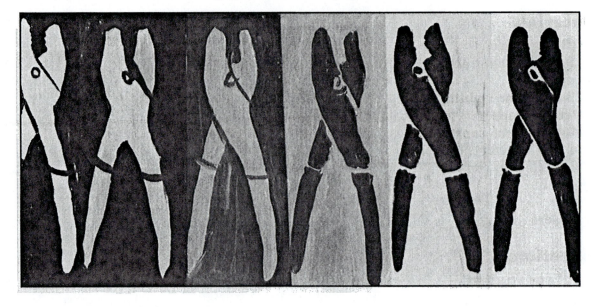

Materials

- assorted keys, tools, or art equipment for visual reference
- 4-by-6-inch tagboard
- 6-by-24-inch white paper
- black and white tempera paint
- paint trays
- paintbrushes
- pencil
- ruler
- scissors

Directions

Have students:

1. On 4-by-6-inch tagboard, draw an object, making the object as large as the tagboard.

2. Cut out to create a template.

3. Using a pencil and a ruler, divide a sheet of 6-by-24-inch white paper into six 4-by-6-inch rectangles.

4. Trace the template into each rectangle.

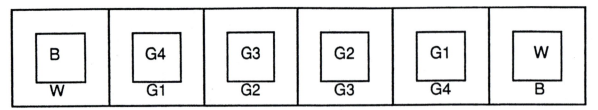

5. In box 1, paint the object black and the background white. In box 6, paint the object white and the background black.

6. In box 2, mix a little black into white to make a light gray for the background (G-1). Use the same color for the object in box 5.

7. Mix a little more black into white for a slightly darker gray (G-2). Use this color in box 3 for the background and in box 4 for the object .

8. Create colors G-3 and G-4 in a similar fashion (slightly darker gray each time) and paint using the figure as a reference. The object will change value gradually from black through grays to white, while the background will change value gradually from white to black.

Design Element: Value—high versus low contrast

Art History: Rembrandt for high versus low contrast

Grade Level: Intermediate

Materials

- 12-by-18-inch construction paper (any color except black, white, or gray)
- crayons or oil pastels (black, white, gray)
- ruler
- pencil
- black felt-tip marker

Directions

Have students:

1. On 12-by-18-inch construction paper, use a ruler to draw *T*'s of various sizes that start at the bottom of the paper and are stacked on top of each other to the top of the paper. Do this until the paper is filled.

2. Connect the *T*'s by extending lines vertically or horizontally (or add vertical and horizontal lines if necessary) so that squares and rectangles are formed.

3. Using a black felt-tip marker and a ruler, trace over the lines.

4. Starting in one of the squares or rectangles, color one edge of the shape with either white, black, or gray. Start out by pressing very hard and gradually lessen the pressure to the other edge of the shape, making a value scale in each shape. (For an added challenge, some shapes may be colored on one side, some on two sides, some on three sides, and some on all four sides. No matter what color, start coloring by pressing very hard and gradually lessen the pressure as you cross the shape.) Try not to have the same color side by side; therefore, some shapes may be left blank, but try not to have two blank spaces side by side. The same value shape or two blank shapes may touch at corners.

Design Element: Value—achromatic value scales; Composition—asymmetrical

Art History: Rembrandt for value variation; Mondrian for asymmetrical omposition

Grade Level: Intermediate

Materials

- 12-by-18-inch practice paper
- still-life objects
- 12-by-18-inch white drawing paper
- black felt-tip pen
- pencil
- ruler

Directions

Have students:

1. On 12-by-18-inch pracice paper, draw any three objects in the classroom. Draw the objects large to create a balanced 12-by-18-inch composition.

2. At a window, light source (i.e., light table), or with carbon paper, transfer the design to 12-by-18-inch white drawing paper.

3. Draw a 1-by-1-inch grid over the entire composition using a pencil and a ruler.

4. (Option: Outline the drawing with a black felt-tip marker). In the squares that contain the objects, use a black felt-tip pen to draw two types of crosshatch lines (choose from horizontal, vertical, 45-degree diagonals). Side-by-side squares must not have the same combination of lines.

5. In the background, draw one type of hatching (lines that do not cross) lines in each shape, and again be sure that two squares side by side are not the same.

Design Element: Value—crosshatching and hatching lines to show decorative value

Art History: Dürer for crosshatching and hatching lines

Grade Level: Intermediate

Materials

- 12-by-18-inch practice paper
- 12-by-18-inch charcoal paper
- chalk or color pencils (black, white, gray)
- shiny kitchen objects for visual reference
- spray fixative

- 12-by-18-inch white drawing paper
- 12-by-18-inch construction paper
- black marker
- scissors
- pencil
- ruler

Directions

Have students:

1. On 12-by-18-inch practice paper, draw a kitchen object (or any shiny object) as large as the paper.

2. Outline the white shapes, black shapes, and then the gray shapes.

3. At a window, light source (i.e., light table), or with carbon paper, transfer the design onto 12-by-18-inch charcoal paper as lightly as possible.

4. Use black, white, and gray chalk or color pencils to blend in the value shapes. Create soft edges and sharp edges.

5. Spray with fixative and cut out the kitchen object.

6. On a sheet of 12-by-18-inch white construction paper, draw a horizontal line lengthwise somewhere above the center of the paper.

7. Place a dot, a vanishing point, at the top center edge of the paper and mark off every two inches along the line drawn in step 6.

8. Using a ruler, draw one line from the dot (the vanishing point) through each mark and to the bottom of the paper.

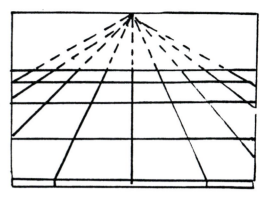

9. Draw horizontal lines below the line drawn in step 6 that gradually get farther apart. In the bottom space, make the lines from the vanishing point vertical to show the edge of the kitchen counter.

10. Color the shapes with black marker like a checkerboard.

11. Cut off the top of the checkerboard (the line drawn in step 6) and glue onto the bottom edge of any color 12-by-18-inch construction paper.

12. Glue the kitchen object onto the counter top.

Design Element: Value—highlight, shadow; Space–one-point perspective

Art History: Rembrandt for values shapes

Grade Level: Upper elementary

Chapter

6

Color

Color offers many areas of study for the art student through its expressive qualities as well as the color relationships on a color wheel. Color can be studied in and of itself or as an additional aspect to a project that exemplifies one of the other design elements. For example, color must be considered when studying the balance of a composition (chapter 1). Lines (chapter 2), areas (chapter 3), and textures (chapter 4) may have color. Colors may have values (chapter 5). Space (chapter 7) can be created through the use of color, and three-dimensional pieces (chapter 8) may have color.

The Color Wheel

With the elementary student, basic knowledge of the *color wheel* and of the terminology associated with it serves as a good starting point. The term *hue* is used with specific colors. Each variation of a color is correctly called a *hue* of that color. The lightness or darkness of a color is referred to as its *value*. However, I have found that students have a better understanding of the value of a color when the terms *tint* and *shade* are used to describe a color. A tint is a color with white added, and a *shade* is a color with black added. *Intensity* is the purity of a color. When another color is added, that color lessens the intensity of the original color. The concept of *tones*, the mixture of *complementary* colors, may serve as a springboard for studying intensity. When complementary colors, colors that are opposite on the color wheel, are mixed, the intensity of each color is neutralized or toned down. In fact, the equal mixture of any two *complements* plus white will create a gray. Additionally, a flesh tone may be made by mixing any two *complements* with white. For example, orange plus a little blue and white results in a flesh tone, as does yellow plus violet and white, as does red plus green and white.

Primary, Secondary, and Tertiary Colors

Other *color wheel* terminology that may be the basis of a project can begin with the study of the *primary* colors– red, yellow, and blue. The work of Piet Mondrian, *Composition with Red, Blue, and Yellow*, may serve as a project idea through his balance of rectangles and squares painted in red, yellow, and blue. From the mixture of primary colors, the student may create any color; however, two colors cannot be mixed together to create a primary color. The mixture of two primary colors results in the *secondary* colors—orange, green, and violet. Mixing a neighboring primary color and a secondary color creates the *tertiary* colors—red-orange, yellow-orange, yellow-green, blue-green, blue-violet, and red-violet. Victor Vasarely's *Vonal-Ksz* incorporates the many varying *hues* one can achieve through the mixtures of primary, secondary, and tertiary colors.

Color Relationships

The *relationships of colors* on the color wheel may serve as the springboard for an assignment. *Analogous* colors, colors that are neighbors on the color wheel, will always afford a pleasing color combination. The paintings of the Rouen Cathedral by Claude

Monet incorporate analogous colors. **Triadic** colors, colors that form a triangle on the color wheel, will relay an expressive quality. For example, a project may consist of the student drawing the same clown face twice. One of the faces will be painted with one set of triadic colors—red, yellow, and blue, for example—while the other face will be painted with another set, orange, green, and violet. The student will readily see that the triadic colors affect the expressive qualities of the same clown face. Emil Nolde, an Expressionist, incorporated the use of triadic colors into his religious painting *The Last Supper*.

In Picasso's Rose and Blue Periods, the student can see the use of another color relationship called **monochromatic**, that is, **tints**, **tones**, and **shades** of one color. Monet's serial paintings of the Rouen Cathedral show his incorporation of **warm** and **cool** colors. Warm colors consist of reds, oranges, and yellows while cool colors are blues, greens, and violets. Not only do warm and cool colors denote a season of the year, but they also create the illusion of depth. Warm colors will make an object appear closer in a composition while cool colors appear to make the objects recede into the picture plane. Victor Vasarely incorporates this spatial illusion created through the use of warm and cool colors in many of his paintings that consist of geometric shapes such as *Vonal-Ksz*.

Simultaneous Contrast

Simultaneous contrast refers to an optical illusion created by color and the color sensors in ours eyes called cones. For example, when one first comes into a room after being outside in the bright sunshine, the room will appear very dark at first even if the lights are on. The same happens when one views predominately one color. When one looks at green objects and then looks away, everything else appears more red for a few moments. The cones in the eyes are adjusting in terms of **complementary** colors. Jasper Johns's *Flags* is an excellent example of **simultaneous contrast**.

Local Colors

Local colors relate to the actual colors that make up an object. For example, a banana's **local** colors may seem to be yellow. Upon closer inspection, one will observe that a banana also contains browns, yellow-greens, and a variety of hues of yellow. The Photo-realist work of Richard Estes's *Central Savings* provides excellent examples of an artist who recorded the local colors of urban scenes through careful observation.

Color and Space

The illusion of **space** and depth through the use of colors is called **atmospheric perspective**. The illusion may be created by lessening the intensity of a color on objects that one wants to appear farther away in a scene. In a landscape scene, the colors will appear to be lighter and grayer in the distance. The humidity in the atmosphere will tone down colors. Even the sky will be a lighter tone of blue closer to the horizon. The landscape painting *The Buffalo Trail* by Alfred Bierstadt offers an amazing example of atmospheric perspective.

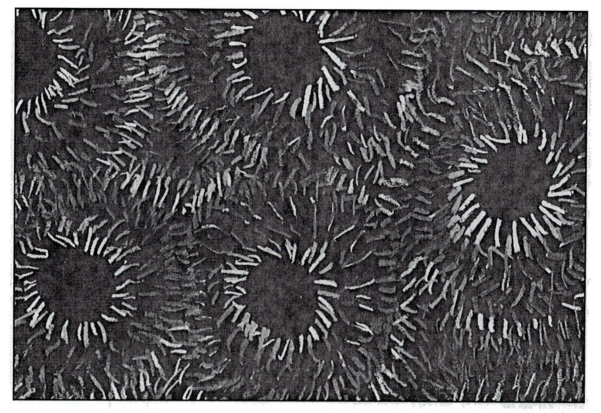

Materials

- 12-by-18-inch black construction paper
- oil pastels (red, orange, yellow, green, blue, violet)
- 3-inch-diameter tagboard circle template

Directions

Have students:

1. Trace the circle (using the yellow oil pastel) template five times onto 12-by-18-inch black construction paper by drawing yellow lines that go off the edge of the circle template. Do not trace the shape with a solid line. Use rays of lines. Make small yellow rays close together around each circle.

2. Next use orange to make marks short, close together, and overlapped into the yellow marks.

3. When rays "bump" into each other from two circles, rays "bounce" to next circle.

4. Continue making rays around each circle following the colors of the color wheel. After green, start over with yellow. Continue to the edge of paper until rays fill the entire paper.

Design Element: Color—color wheel

Art History: Van Gogh's *Starry Night* for lines of color

Grade Level: Lower primary

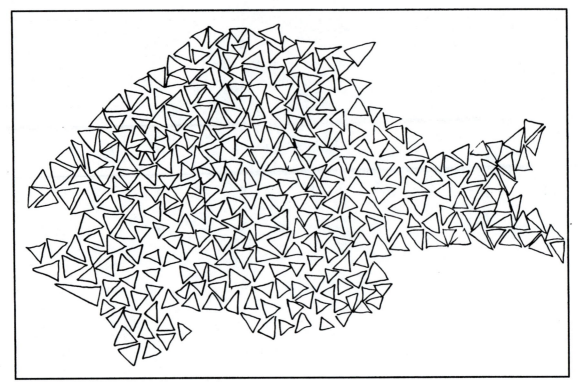

Materials

- 12-by-18-inch practice paper
- 12-by-18-inch black construction paper
- 12-by-18-inch white construction paper (or strips of red, orange, yellow, green, blue, and violet construction paper)
- tempera paint (red, yellow, blue)
- scissors
- paintbrush
- glue
- pencil

Directions

Have students:

1. On 12-by-18-inch practice paper, draw a silhouette of a fish that fills the entire paper. (This activity works well with any silhouette shape—butterfly, dinosaur, bird, etc.)

2. Cut out and trace onto 12-by-18-inch black construction paper.

3. Cut small triangles from strips of yellow, orange, red, violet, blue, and green construction paper.

   Option: On white construction paper, squirt out yellow, red, blue, and yellow paint. Place yellow at the top, then red, then blue, and yellow at the bottom of the paper. Blend by starting at the top and working down to create the blended colors of the rainbow (always start blending at the top; do not go back up or the colors will become muddied).

4. Start at either the tail or head, and glue in the yellow triangles. End on the opposite side with green. Be sure to follow the colors of the rainbow.

Design Element: Color—color theory: mixing of primaries to produce secondary colors; Area—silhouetted shapes

Art History: Roman and Byzantine mosaics for color shapes

Grade Level: Lower primary

Materials

- 4-inch tall precut numbers (or an Ellison machine may be used to make stencils)
- 12-by-18-inch white construction paper
- watercolor paint
- paintbrush
- black marker
- 12-by-18-inch black construction paper
- scissors
- pencil
- glue

Directions

Have students:

1. Trace numbers onto 12-by-18-inch white construction paper to make an asymmetrical design. Remember to overlap a number only once in one spot.

2. Outline numbers with black marker.

3. Paint the numbers where they do not overlap with red, blue, or yellow. Two numbers of the same color should not overlap.

4. Where the numbers are overlapped, paint the secondary color (i.e., red over yellow will be orange, red over blue will be violet, and blue over yellow will be green).

5. Cut out numbers and glue onto 12-by-18-inch black construction paper.

Design Element: Color—primary and secondary colors; Composition—asymmetrical balance

Art History: Stuart Davis for compositions using primary and secondary colors

Grade Level: Lower primary

Size Variation Design

Materials

- any object for subject matter
- 12-by-18-inch practice paper
- 12-by-18-inch white construction paper
- black marker
- watercolor paint
- paintbrush
- pencil

Directions

Have students:

1. On 12-by-18-inch practice paper, draw one object at least three or more times, but a different size each time. Draw them so they touch the edges of the paper and so that they overlap.

2. On the paper, determine where three analogous colors will be painted. The same color should not touch side by side, but may touch at a corner.

3. At a window, light source (i.e., light table), or with carbon paper, transfer the design onto 12-by-18-inch white construction paper.

4. Paint the shapes and the background, referring to drawing from step 2.

5. Carefully outline the design with black marker.

Design Element: Color—analogous colors; Composition—asymmetrical balance

Art History: Edgar Degas and Henri de Toulouse-Lautrec for asymmetrical balance; Picasso's Blue Period for analogous colors

Grade Level: Intermediate

Materials

- 12-by-18-inch tagboard
- 3-by-3-inch tagboard
- oil pastels
- black tempera paint, slightly diluted
- paintbrush
- pencil
- scissors
- ruler

Directions

Have students:

1. On 3-by-3-inch tagboard, draw a leaf that touches all four edges of the paper.

2. Cut out the leaf shape.

3. Using a ruler and a pencil, mark off a grid of 3-by-3-inch squares on the 12-by-18-inch tagboard.

4. At a window, light source (i.e., light table), or with carbon paper, transfer leaf into each square, the same way each time.

5. Color leaves with oil pastel in a repeating design of three "fall" colors (red, orange, yellow, gold, or brown). Leave a gap for the veins.

6. Color the background blue or green, but the blue or green should not touch the leaves. Leave a gap between the leaf and the blue or green.

7. Apply one coat of slightly diluted black tempera paint. (Have students dip the paintbrush in water before dipping into the tempera paint—this will help the oil pastel "resist" the tempera paint.)

Design Element: Color—fall colors; Composition—repetition

Art History: Warhol for asymmetrical composition; Claude Monet for colors of the seasons

Grade Level: Intermediate

The Kitchen Sink

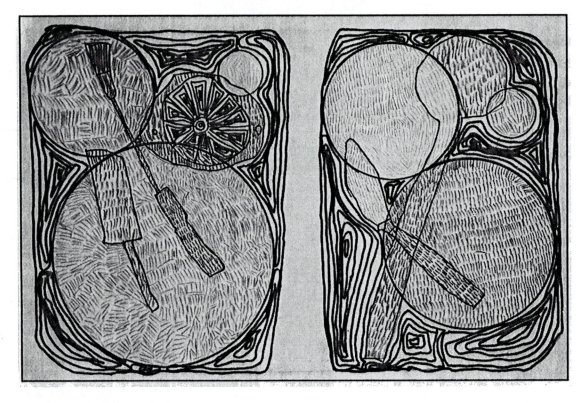

Materials

- kitchen utensils for visual reference
- 12-by-18-inch drawing paper
- color pencils
- black fine-tip pen
- 6 circle templates of varying sizes (lids work well)
- pencil

Directions

Have students:

1. Draw a contour line drawing of five different kitchen utensils.

2. Outline using a black fine-tip pen.

3. To represent the sink, draw a line ½ inch from each edge of the paper. The corners should be rounded.

4. Trace six circles of varying size onto the design. Trace the circles in a balanced arrangement.

5. Outline using a black fine-tip pen.

6. With color pencil, each circle will be filled with short lines of one color, but each shape in the circle must be a different hue of that color. Each circle will be one of the primary or secondary colors. If the kitchen objects are not covered by a circle, draw in short lines with a gray pencil.

7. With a black felt pen, fill the negative areas with contour lines that go around the objects and the circles.

Design Element: Color—hues; Area—proportion and scale; Line—contour lines

Art History: Monet for hues

Grade Level: Intermediate

Materials

- compass
- 12-by-18-inch white drawing paper
- 12-by-18-inch black construction paper
- markers, all colors
- scissors
- pencil
- glue

Directions

Have students:

1. On 12-by-18-inch white paper, use a compass to make at least five bullseyes that overlap. Each bullseye should have an odd number of lines. Once two bullseyes overlap, do not draw a third bullseye through the overlap area.

2. Using a primary color (red, yellow, or blue), color every other space between the lines. One bullseye is one primary color. Two bullseyes of the same color should not overlap. Do not color the overlapped areas.

3. Where two colors overlap, decide which secondary color will be made by their mixture (i.e., red over yellow will be orange, red over blue will be violet, and blue over yellow will be green). Color the secondary color in the shapes where two bullseyes overlap.

4. Cut out the bullseyes design and mount on 12-by-18-inch black construction paper.

Design Element: Color—primary and secondary colors

Art History: Stella for compositions using bullseyes

Grade Level: Intermediate

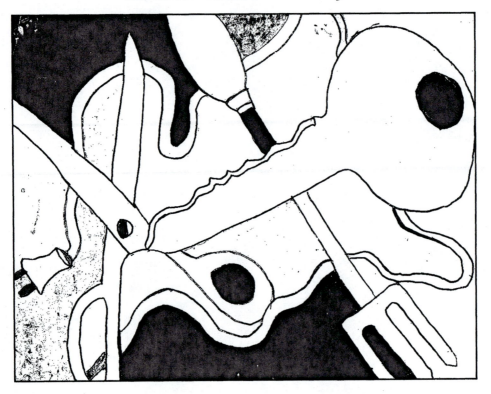

Materials

- classroom still-life objects
- 12-by-18-inch practice paper
- 12-by-18-inch white construction paper
- tempera paint, all colors
- paintbrush
- black marker
- pencil

Directions

Have students:

1. Draw three different objects from the classroom on 12-by-18-inch practice paper. Draw the objects large enough to fill the entire paper. Overlap the objects, but show transparency. For a balanced asymmetrical composition, the objects should touch each edge of the paper.

2. At a window, light source (i.e., light table), or with carbon paper, transfer the design to 12-by-18-inch white construction paper.

3. Paint the shapes with tempera paint using one of the monochromatic colors, tints, tones, and shades of one color, listed below:

   red plus white, black, and/or green
   blue plus white, black, and/or orange
   yellow plus white, black, and/or violet

   orange plus white, black, and/or violet
   green plus white, black, and/or red
   violet plus white, black, and/or yellow

4. Outline the shapes with black marker as neatly as possible. All outlining lines should be the same width.

Design Element: Color—monochromatic colors;
Area—silhouette shapes; Composition—asymmetrical balance

Art History: Picasso's Blue Period for monochromatic colors

Grade Level: Intermediate

Materials

- 9-by-12-inch drawing paper
- color pencils
- 9-by-12-inch black construction paper
- pencil
- scissors
- glue
- ruler

Directions

Have students:

1. Draw each letter of their names in block letters on 9-by-12-inch paper. Use the width of a ruler so all letters will have the same width. Each letter should touch one edge of the paper and overlap another letter.

2. Where letters do not overlap, draw vertical lines with color pencils using the primary colors (red, blue, yellow). Each letter should be one of the primary colors. Two letters of the same color should not overlap.

3. Where letters overlap, draw vertical lines of the appropriate secondary colors. If three letters overlap in one spot, use black or gray. Red plus yellow will be orange, yellow plus blue will be green, and red plus blue will be violet.

4. Cut out the letters and glue onto 9-by-12-inch black construction paper.

Design Element: Color—primary and secondary colors

Art History: Davis for compositions using primary and secondary colors

Grade Level: Intermediate

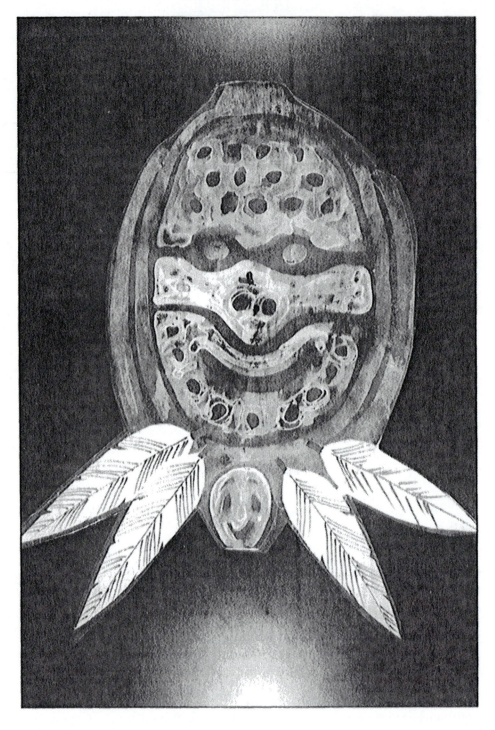

Materials

- visual references of Eskimo masks
- 12-by-18-inch practice paper
- 12-by-18-inch tagboard
- tempera paint
- paintbrush
- India ink (this ink is permanent when spilled; have students bring in old shirts to wear when doing this project)
- tan manila paper
- sink
- glue
- pencil
- scissors
- construction paper
- option: jute

Directions

Have students:

1. On 12-by-18-inch practice paper, draw a symmetrical or asymmetrical mask using features of animals and humans referring to the visual references of Eskimo masks. Include outside bands and appendages.

2. At a window, light source (i.e., light table), or with carbon paper, transfer to 12-by-18-inch tagboard.

3. Paint using complementary colors (choose: orange and blue, red and green, or yellow and violet). Add any amount of white. Do not use complementary colors by themselves. Leave a gap between the colors (colors should not touch). Let dry.

4. Brush India ink over entire surface. Let dry.

5. Place the tagboard in a sink and gently brush off India ink as water runs over the design. (The colors will appear weathered.)

6. Cut out the mask and attach fur, feathers, or both. Feathers can be made with a brown marker on tan manila paper. Fur can be made by using use jute and unraveling it.

Design Element: Color—color theory: complementary colors

Art History: Eskimo masks for tones of colors

Grade Level: Upper elementary

Caran D'Ache Tennis Shoe

Materials

- 12-by-18-inch practice paper
- 12-by-18-inch tagboard
- tennis shoes for visual reference
- Caran D'Ache or water-soluble crayons
- small paintbrush
- black felt-tip pen
- scissors
- pencil
- glue
- 12-by-18-inch construction paper, any color

Directions

Have students:

1. Draw a tennis shoe on 12-by-18-inch practice paper, filling the entire paper. Draw the shapes and the stitch marks.

2. Trace the design to 12-by-18-inch tagboard.

3. Color around the shapes with Caran D'Ache or water-soluble crayon.

4. Pull the color into the shape with a small paintbrush and water.

5. Color the stitches and outline the shapes with a black felt-tip pen.

6. Cut out shoe and mount on construction paper.

Design Element: Color—color shapes

Art History: Warhol's silkscreens for color shapes

Grade Level: Upper elementary

Materials

- 12-by-18-inch white construction paper
- ruler
- markers, all colors
- pencil

Directions

Have students:

1. On 12-by-18-inch paper, have students draw their initials to fill the entire paper (divide the paper every six inches– each letter will be 6 by 12 inches).

2. Draw six horizontal lines to make three stripes.

3. Color the first letter red where it is not overlapped by a stripe.

4. Color the second letter yellow where it is not overlapped by a stripe.

5. Color the third letter blue where it is not overlapped by a stripe.

6. Color the top stripe red where it is not overlapped by a letter.

7. Color the middle stripe yellow where it is not overlapped by a letter.

8. Color the bottom stripe blue where it is not overlapped by a letter.

9. Using the following formulas, color in the correct secondary color where the letters and stripes overlap:

red	blue	blue
+yellow	+red	+ yellow
———	———	———
orange	violet	green

10. Outline the letters and stripes with a black marker.

Design Element: Color—primary and secondary colors

Art History: Franz Marc for compositions using primary and secondary colors

Grade Level: Upper elementary

Materials

- yucca pods (or plastic flowers) for visual reference
- crayons
- India ink (this ink leaves a permanent stain; have students bring in old shirts to wear when doing this project)
- paintbrush
- 12-by-18-inch practice paper
- 12-by-18-inch tagboard
- 12-by-18-inch construction paper
- X-ACTO knife, needles, or stylus*
- glue
- color pencils
- scissors
- pencil

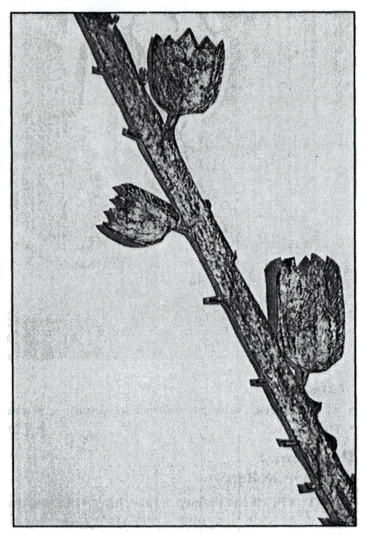

Directions

Have students:

1. Draw a yucca pod with a stem on 12-by-18-inch practice paper. Draw the pod very large and concentrate on the shape of the yucca plant and its highlights and shadows.

2. With pencil, outline the light, medium, and dark areas seen on the surface of the yucca pod.

3. Trace to 12-by-18-inch tagboard using pencil.

4. Choose three crayon colors that clash (discordant colors).

5. Color the design. Use one of the colors in the dark areas, one in the medium areas, and one in the light areas. Color hard.

6. Color the entire pod and stem with tan or brown crayon. Color very hard.

7. Scratch the detail lines of the yucca pod into the crayon with an X-ACTO knife, needle, or stylus.

8. Brush the tagboard with India ink.

9. Buff or rub hard immediately after application of India ink (if it dries, the ink will be very hard to rub off).

---

*Review with students safety precautions in using knives. Cut away from your hand. Do not walk around with the knife. Have cardboard underneath. Do not talk while cutting. Knives are not toys.

10. To create a silhouette shape of the yucca pod and branch, cut out the yucca pod and branch and trace onto a sheet of 12-by-18-inch construction paper that is one of the colors of crayon used to color the yucca pod.

11. Cut out and glue the silhouette shape onto a piece of 12-by-18-inch construction paper that is a color of one of the crayons used in the yucca pod, but not the same color as the silhouette shape.

12. Glue the yucca and branch ½ inch to the right or left of the silhouette shape.

Design Element: Color—discordant colors (colors that clash); Value—value shapes

Art History: Matisse; Fauvism for discordant colors

Grade Level: Upper elementary

Still-Life Painting

Materials

- classroom still-life objects
- 12-by-18-inch practice paper
- 12-by-18-inch tagboard
- tempera paint
- paintbrush
- India ink (this ink leaves a permanent stain; have students bring in old shirts to wear when doing this project)
- sink
- pencil

Directions

Have students:

1. On 12-by-18-inch practice paper, draw three objects in the classroom that are free-standing. Make the objects overlap but show opaqueness.

2. Draw a table line that is approximately ½ the height of the tallest object.

3. Trace the design onto 12-by-18-inch tagboard.

4. Choose a base color to be mixed with every color you plan to use. Do not use black. (A wide variety of hues will be created off the base color.)

5. Paint each object one color plus the base color (e.g., an object will be yellow plus the base color of blue). Variation: Looks great when students add varying amounts of white. Apply the paint thickly. Leave a ¼-inch gap between each color shape (to create a black outline).

6. Let paint dry for 24 hours.

7. Brush the entire painting with India ink. Let dry.

8. Place the painting in a sink. Gently brush the painting while water is gently running over it.

9. Let dry.

Design Element: Color—color mixtures; Space—overlap

Art History: Georges Rouault for use of black outlines and hues

Grade Level: Upper elementary

Chapter

7

Space

The design element of **space** deserves study even though all the previous design elements may create the illusion of space. For example, the student has studied that space can be created by using converging lines or by analyzing the areas of highlights and shadows on a glass object. Furthermore, bold textures will appear closer than small, fine textures within a scene, while values on a surface create the illusion of volume. With color, the use of atmospheric perspective affords the illusion of space in a landscape scene. All of these design elements basically portray the distance between objects or the three-dimensional quality of objects on a two-dimensional surface. The challenge to represent a three-dimensional world on a flat surface may become more understandable to the student when the tools to show space are explored.

Space is perceived by **stereoscopic sight** and **kinesthetic sight**. Stereoscopic sight refers to the slightly different views that each eye perceives, which are then combined by the brain. The combination of the two slightly different views allows one to perceive space or three-dimensional objects. View Masters incorporate this feature so one can sense space in its scenes. Kinesthetic sight pertains to the fact that one's eyes can only focus on one object at a time—objects in the peripheral vision appear blurry. The student must decide whether to incorporate this concept into a composition: all the objects in the picture plane might be in focus or the objects in the distance or on the edges of the composition might be blurred by using soft edges. A comparison of the works of Richard Estes's *Central Savings* with Joseph Mallord William Turner's *The Slave Ship* may help illustrate this concept.

Decorative Space

For the younger student, the use of *decorative* space affords an excellent starting point. By drawing cubes or converging lines or geometric shapes across a picture plane, one can create the illusion of a dimensional surface. The work of Al Held serves as an example of the decorative use of space.

Ways to Show Space

Students at the third-grade level are ready to understand and incorporate the illusion of space into their art projects. The following ways to show space, or depth, offer many opportunities for exciting art projects for the elementary student.

Size and Position

Size and **position** offer an introduction to the illusion of space for the beginning art student. If one wants to make an object appear closer to the viewer than another object, one simply draws the closer object larger than the other. For example, the varying sizes of the figures in Georges Seurat's *A Sunday Afternoon on the Island of La Grande Jatte* create the illusion of space. The viewer's mind automatically senses that an object is closer if the object is **positioned** or placed lower in the picture plane. By the position of the figures in Raphael's *School of Athens*, the artist has created the illusion of figures moving within a deep space.

Overlap, Transparency, and Interpenetration

The concepts of **overlap**, **transparency**, and **interpenetration** assist the student in portraying the distance between objects, whether the objects are some distance from each other, very close together, or even penetrating each other. Overlap consists of drawing one object in front of the other so that the second object is partially hidden. The work of early Italian Renaissance artist Giotto's *Madonna Enthroned* overlaps figures to create the illusion of space. Cubism artists Braque and Picasso created the illusion of shallow space by using transparency, one sees through the objects, and shapes of colors to portray their subject matter. The space shown with **transparency** appears very shallow. In fact, the viewer sometimes cannot perceive which object is closer and which object is farther in the distance because the objects appear to be on the same plane. Picasso's *Ambroise Vollard* incorporates **transparency**. The concept of interpenetration causes the viewer to sense that objects are penetrating or going through each other. Frank Stella's *Brooklyn Bridge* incorporates lines of colors that appear to pass in and out of each other.

Fractional Space and Ambiguous Space

Fractional space and **ambiguous space** offer the student the opportunity to manipulate and distort space on a two-dimensional surface. Fractional space, portraying more than one view of an object at one time, was used by the Egyptians and by Pablo Picasso to represent the human figure. For example, the Egyptians combined a frontal view of the eye with a profile view of the head. Similarly, during Picasso's Abstract Period, he would combine a front view and a profile of a face within one figure, as seen in *Grande Tete de Femme au Chapeau Orné*. With ambiguous space, objects are placed together in a scene where they cannot possibly exist together in reality, or the objects' proportion and scale are distorted. The work of René Magritte masterfully uses ambiguous space to create surrealistic fantasy scenes that initially appear real. William Hogarth's frontispiece *Kirby's Perspective* uses ambiguous space for humorous effect.

Converging Parallels

One of the most common means to show space involves the use of **converging parallels** (a study of converging parallels can serve as an introduction to geometric perspective, below). The term *converging parallels* may seem to be an oxymoron, but it offers the student a visual "trick of the trade" to create the illusion of space on a two-dimensional surface. For example, the younger student usually will draw a road going off into the distance by using two parallel lines. To create the illusion of the road receding into the distance, the lines should gradually come together, converging at some point in the picture plane or appearing as if they would converge at some point beyond the picture plane.

Geometric Perspective

Geometric perspective, comprising **one-point**, **two-point**, and **three-point perspective**, incorporates converging parallels, but in a more precise manner. Each perspective has specific rules for the lines and how they relate to a *vanishing point* where lines converge. For example, one-point perspective implies that the viewer is standing in front of an object and sees the sides or edges of the object receding. A simple illustration would be a road going off into the distance. In one-point perspective, the sides of the road meet at a vanishing point on the horizon line. In one-point perspective, all lines are either vertical, horizontal, or go to the vanishing point. Maurice Utrillo's *Sacré Coeur, Monmartre et Rue Saint Rustique* uses one-point perspective. Two-point and three-point perspective (which are too advanced for the elementary student) imply that the viewer is standing at a "corner" of an object and sees the sides (width and depth) of the object receding into the distance. Consequently, two-point perspective places two vanishing points on the horizon line. In two-point perspective, all lines are either vertical or go to one of the two vanishing points. Salvador Dali's *The Crucifixion* dramatically uses two-point perspective to portray the cross. Three-point perspective implies that the viewer is again standing at a "corner" of an object and observes the lines of the sides (width and depth) of the object receding toward two vanishing points on the horizon line. However, with three-point perspective, all lines that would be vertical in reality recede to a third vanishing point at the top of the picture plane. All lines in three-point perspective must go to one of the three vanishing points. Photographs of skyscrapers taken at eye level show three-point perspective.

Materials

- tempera paint (white, red)
- paintbrush
- 12-by-18-inch green construction paper
- 12-by-18-inch brown construction paper
- 18-by-24-inch light blue or gray construction paper (if 18-by-24-inch paper is not available, use 9-by-12-inch for the green and brown and 12-by-18-inch for the light blue or gray)
- 1-by-2-inch piece of corrugated cardboard
- black marker
- scissors
- glue

Directions

Have students:

1. Using a 1-by-2-inch piece of corrugated cardboard, dip an edge in white tempera paint to print by using repeated dabs. For the tree, make dabs on brown paper in a *Y* shape by starting at the bottom of the paper and continuing to the outer edges. For an evergreen tree, dab on green construction paper by printing upside down *V*'s that start at the top of the paper and get wider towards the bottom of the paper.

2. Cut out the evergreen tree first. Cut out skinny *V*'s along the edges to show the branches.

3. Glue down the evergreen tree somewhere in the middle of the light blue or gray construction paper. Do not glue it along the bottom edge.

4. Cut out the brown tree.

5. Glue down the brown tree so that it overlaps the evergreen and the base of the trunk is lower than the lowest part of the evergreen tree.

6. Dab snow on the ground using the corrugated cardboard and white tempera paint.

7. Draw in birds using circles and *V*'s.

8. Paint the birds with red tempera paint and then outline with black marker.

Design Element: Space—shown by position and overlap

Art History: Ruisdael for landscapes showing position and overlap

Grade Level: Lower primary

Materials

- 18-by-24-inch white construction paper or butcher paper
- tempera paint
- paintbrush
- black marker
- pencil

Directions

Have students:

1. Have students trace their hands and feet onto 18-by-24-inch white construction or butcher paper. Be sure the hands and toes are pointing to the top of the paper.

2. Between the hands and the feet, draw a head and torso using a circle and two over-lapped triangles.

3. For arms draw L-shaped lines from the hands to the shoulders. Be sure the lines converge, that is, get closer together as they get closer to the shoulders.

4. Turn the paper upside down to draw the legs. Start with the heel to draw an L-shaped line to the hips. The second L-shaped line should start from the middle of the foot and continue to the hip.

5. Draw in face, hair, and patterned clothes for boy or girl.

6. Paint the figure with tempera paint.

7. Paint the background blue for the sky.

8. Outline figure with a black marker.

Design Element: Space—shown by size, converging parallels, and foreshortening

Art History: Michelangelo; Caravaggio for foreshortening (converging lines on a human figure)

Grade Level: Lower primary and up

Materials

- 12-by-18-inch white construction paper
- crayons
- paintbrush
- watercolor paint
- pencil

Directions

Have students:

1. On a 12-by-18-inch handout with lightly pre-drawn ovals (including eye line, nose line, and mouth line), have the students draw their profiles using the following steps:

   a. Draw the forehead with a curved line from the top of the oval to the eye line.
   b. Draw the nose from the eye line to the nose line.
   c. Draw the lips with an m-shaped line on the lip line.
   d. Draw the chin with a U-shaped line from the lips to the bottom of the oval.
   e. Draw the profile eye with a sideways *V* and a *C*.

2. Draw front view:

   a. Draw the eyes with *C*'s—one should be "doing push ups" and the other should be "lying on its back."
   b. Draw the nostril with a *C* and an *O*.
   c. Draw the lips with a sideways *V* and a sideways *I*.

3. Draw the eyebrows.

4. Draw the ears with *C*'s.

5. Draw the jaw line with a large *U*.

6. Draw the neck with a line that begins from underneath the ears.

7. Draw the shoulders and collar.

8. Draw hair. Remember that the hair goes from the ears to above the skull line.

9. Trace over lines of the face with black crayon.

10. With crayon, color in each shape with a different line in any color but black.

    Each shape is a different color and type of line.

11. With watercolor, paint each shape with a wash that is a different color than the crayon lines.

Design Element: Space—fractional space; Area—facial proportions; Line—line variety

Art History: Picasso's *Portrait of a Young Girl* for fractional space

Grade Level: Lower primary through intermediate

Forest Floor

Materials

- three sheets of 3-by-5-inch tagboard
- visual references of leaves
- 9-by-12-inch watercolor paper
- Caran D'Ache or water-soluble crayons
- paintbrush
- scissors
- pencil

Directions

Have students:

1. On each 3-by-5-inch tagboard, draw a leaf, entirely filling the tagboard. Each piece of tagboard should have a different leaf.

2. Cut out the leaves.

3. Trace the leaves onto 9-by-12-inch watercolor paper, showing overlap of at least 15 leaves.

4. Use "fall" colors of Caran D'Ache or water-soluble crayon (red, yellow, gold, orange, brown) to outline the leaf and a different fall color to color the veins. Change the color combination for each leaf.

5. Use green and dark green Caran D'Ache or water-soluble crayon to make grass lines in the background.

6. With a small paintbrush and water, carefully brush over the lines so the Caran D'Ache or water-soluble crayon dissolves. Brush inward on the leaves. Keep background colors in the background.

Design Element: Space—overlap

Art History: Giotto and Early Renaissance painting for overlap

Grade Level: Intermediate

Materials

- map of school's attendance area
- 12-by-18-inch watercolor paper
- Caran D'Ache or water-soluble crayons
- black tempera paint
- paintbrush
- pencil

Directions

Have students:

1. Have students find their homes on the street map.

2. On 12-by-18-inch watercolor paper, draw your neighborhood streets, without houses, as a bird would see them flying over. Draw your streets about one inch wide. Continue until the paper is filled.

3. Choose three analogous colors of Caran D'Ache or water-soluble crayon to color in the "yards." Use random shapes of colors.

4. Brush water over the colors so that they blend.

5. Paint the streets black with tempera paint. Remember to keep the streets one inch wide and to paint straight edges by "pulling" the brush in one direction.

Design Element: Space—aerial perspective

Art History: Klee for his use of black lines

Grade Level: Intermediate

Colorado Landscape
(or adapt for any geographic location)

Materials

- three sheets 6-by-18-inch watercolor paper
- watercolor paint
- paintbrush (1-inch flat recommended)

- spray water bottle
- masking tape
- glue

Directions

Have students:

1. Tape a sheet of 6-by-18-inch watercolor paper to the table with masking tape. The tape goes on all four edges.

2. Choose a light, medium, and dark color combination.

3. Spray water onto the paper and dab on the colors (do not brush). This is the "wet on wet" process.

4. Pull the tape off by pulling the tape away from the painting.

5. Tape down the second sheet of watercolor paper.

6. For the "wet on dry" process, the paints are wet but the paper is dry. Brush fat and skinny angle lines that do not crisscross with the same three colors. Carefully pull off the tape.

7. Tape down the third sheet of watercolor paper.

8. For the "dry on dry" process, the paintbrush should have very little paint and water in it and the paper is dry. Make small upward brush strokes with the same three colors.

9. Tear the top edge of the "wet on dry" painting at an angle to create a white edge.

10. Tear the top edge of the "dry on dry" painting with a flowing line.

11. Glue all three paintings together in this order: "wet on wet" for the sky, "wet on dry" for the mountains, and "dry on dry" for the prairie. "Dry on dry" overlaps the "wet on dry"; "wet on dry" overlaps the "wet on wet."

Design Element: Space—hard and soft edges

Art History: Turner for hard and soft edges creating space

Grade Level: Intermediate

Materials

- 6-by-9-inch practice paper
- color markers
- 6-by-9-inch Styrofoam sheets (smooth)
- printer's ink
- brayer
- 6-by-9-inch plexiglass sheet
- 12-by-18-inch white construction paper

- two sheets 6-by-18-inch white construction paper for coral and seaweed
- 12-by-18-inch watercolor paper
- watercolor paint
- paintbrush
- color pencils
- scissors
- glue

Directions

Have students:

1. Draw a fish onto a sheet of 6-by-9-inch practice paper. Be sure to show scales and fins.

2. Use three colors of color markers and decide which lines will be which color.

3. Cut out the fish and trace onto Styrofoam and cut out again.

4. Squirt a dime-size pile of printer's ink onto plexiglass.

5. Roll out the ink using the brayer.

6. With the ink on the brayer, roll the brayer over the Styrofoam.

7. Place the Styrofoam face-down on a sheet of 12-by-18-inch white construction paper and rub firmly so that the ink transfers to the construction paper. Print three or four fish.

8. Wash off the brayer, plexiglass sheet, and Styrofoam.

9. Draw another set of color lines onto your Styrofoam. Refer to chosen colors for lines in step 2. Press firmly.

10. Ink the next color and press over the first fish prints. Make sure the Styrofoam is lined up with your first print.

11. Wash everything.

12. Draw the last set of color lines onto the Styrofoam and print the third color. Let dry.

13. Wash everything.

14. Cut out the fish.

15. Draw the coral on a sheet of 6-by-18-inch construction paper by making topographical lines with color pencils. Use the second piece of 6-by-18-inch construction paper for the seaweed by making S-shaped lines that overlap. Color with markers.

16. Cut out the coral and seaweed.

17. Paint a sheet of 12-by-18-inch watercolor paper with blue and green using the "wet on wet" watercolor technique.

18. Glue fish, seaweed, and coral onto the watercolor paper. Glue them down so it looks like the fish are swimming in and out of the coral and seaweed.

Design Element: Space—overlap (fish going in and out of seaweed), *distinct* versus *diminished details* (fish against watercolor background), converging parallels (topographical lines in the coral).

Art History: Japanese fish prints for *distinct* versus *diminished details*

Grade Level: Intermediate

3-D Crosshatching

Materials

- 12-by-18-inch white drawing paper
- ruler
- black felt-tip pen
- 12-by-18-inch construction paper
- scissors
- glue

Directions

Have students:

1. Choose one of the following three-dimensional shapes.

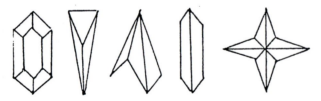

2. On 12-by-18-inch white paper, draw a three-dimensional shape repeatedly using a black felt-tip pen until the shapes touch all four edges. Use a ruler.

3. Fill in each shape with crosshatch lines. Try not to have the same line type side by side. The shapes may be filled with one, two, three, or four crossing lines. Some shapes may be left blank. Use a ruler.

4. Cut out the three-dimensional shapes and glue onto 12-by-18-inch construction paper.

Design Element: Space—illusional

Art History: Vasarely for illusional shapes

Grade Level: Upper elementary

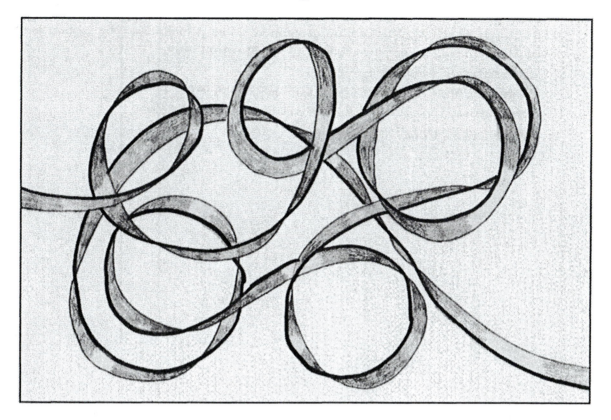

Materials

- 12-by-18-inch white construction paper
- color pencils
- pencil

Directions

Have students:

1. On 12-by-18-inch paper, draw a curving line that overlaps itself several times. Be sure to create a balanced composition.

2. Draw a second line that follows the first line but crosses the first line several times.

3. Draw a third line that will show the thickness of the ribbon—follow one of the lines but never cross that line.

4. Where the ribbon crosses over itself, erase appropriate lines to show overlap.

5. Choose two sets of analogous colors. Each set should have a light, a medium, and a dark color.

6. Starting at one end, proceed along the ribbon: Color one of the shapes or twists with the lightest color in the middle of the shape or twist, the medium color on both sides of the lightest of the light colors, and the darkest color from the medium color to the end of the twist and to the pointed ends (as the ribbon begins

to twist). Use the second set of analogous colors for a new shape or twist. Continue alternating the colors in each twist so it looks like the ribbon is one color on one side and a different color on the other side.

Design Element: Space—converging parallels, overlap

Art History: Baroque and Rococo Art for twisting shapes

Grade Level: Upper elementary

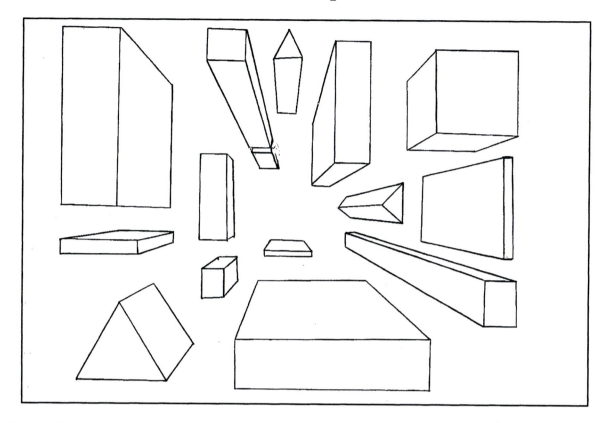

Materials

- 12-by-18-inch white construction paper
- tempera paint
- paintbrush
- pencil
- ruler

Directions

Have students:

1. With a ruler, draw six boxes of any size, anywhere on a sheet of 12-by-18-inch white construction paper.

2. Draw a horizon line across the middle of the paper and place a vanishing point in the center.

3. On each box, draw a line from each corner to the vanishing point. Use a ruler. If the line goes through the box, do not draw it.

4. To draw the back edge of the box, draw lines parallel to the original box in between the vanishing point lines any distance from the original box. Note that these lines must all touch at the corners, that is, the vertical or horizontal lines will meet on the vanishing point lines to create the illusion of a corner.

5. To color the boxes, use the following color theory:

   a. Warm colors appear to come forward. Paint the fronts of boxes that you want to appear closer red, yellow, or orange.
   b. Cool colors appear to recede. Paint the fronts of boxes that you want to appear farther back blue, green, or violet.

c. For tops of boxes, add white to the color you used for the front of the box.
d. For bottoms of boxes, add black to the color you used for the front of the box.
e. For the sides of the boxes, add the complement (the color directly opposite on the color wheel) to the color you used for the front of the box.

6. Paint the background black.

Design Element: Space—one-point perspective

Art History: Vasarely for one-point perspective

Grade Level: Upper elementary

Materials

- 12-by-18-inch white construction paper
- markers
- black felt-tip pen
- ruler
- pencil

Directions

Have students:

1. On 12-by-18-inch white construction paper, draw a vertical line about six inches long from the center of the bottom of the paper.

2. Draw an upside down *U* from the top of the line to the bottom corners of the paper. This will create the bottom of the student's pants leg.

3. Have students draw the front half of the top of their shoes as if they were looking down at them at the top of the upside down *U*.

4. Have students draw three objects on the floor that tell something about them.

5. Mark off every three inches on all four edges. Connect them to make tiles.

6. Color the tiles, shoes, three objects, and pants with marker.

7. Outline with a black felt-tip pen.

Design Element: Space—converging parallels, foreshortening

Art History: Caravaggio; "Uncle Sam Wants You" poster for foreshortening of human figures

Grade Level: Upper elementary

Chapter

8

Three-Dimensional Art

The design element of *three-dimensional art*, or sculpture, affords the student the opportunity to create art that has depth and volume. A greater sense of reality results because one may actually hold or walk around the piece. Three-dimensional art can be created from any material that can be arranged, assembled, carved, or molded into a three-dimensional form.

Three-Dimensional Art and Composition

Three-dimensional art will incorporate one of the four types of *composition* (see chapter 1), that is, the three-dimensional piece will be either *symmetrical*, *asymmetrical*, *repetitive*, or *radial*. The wire sculpture *Variation Within a Sphere, No. 10: The Sun* by Richard Lippold is an example of symmetrical **three-dimensional** art while the sculpture *Saint Peter's Pieta* by Michelangelo represents an asymmetrical form. The decorative relief grillwork from the Carson Pirie Scott Building in Chicago by Louis Sullivan contains repetition of shapes from nature, primarily leaves. An easily accessible example of radial three-dimensional art can be found in the design of a manhole cover.

Ways to Create Three-Dimensional Art

Three dimensional art may be created through the processes of *subtraction, manipulation, addition,* and *substitution*. The process of subtraction consists of carving to remove material. For example, Michelangelo said that to release the figure he saw within a piece of marble he simply carved away the marble he did not need. This process can be very unforgiving—carving away too much is what the professional artist refers to as a major "oops." The manipulation process consists of reshaping or rearranging a medium. The pinch pot may be classified as three-dimensional art created through manipulation because the student simply reshapes a lump of clay to create a pinch pot. Pottery thrown on a potter's wheel is also art created through manipulation because the potter is rearranging a piece of clay. Sculpture by addition involves assembling material or materials into a three-dimensional form. Toothpick and marshmallow structures may be classified as sculptures created by addition, as well as Louise Nevelson's *Royal Tide #1*. The substitution process involves the use of a mold to create art. Auguste Rodin's *The Thinker* was cast from a mold.

Three-Dimensional Art and the Other Design Elements

In the process of creating three-dimensional art, the student will consider all of the previous design elements. As stated earlier, all three-dimensional art has one of the four compositional forms. Additionally, three-dimensional art may incorporate *line*, *area*, *texture*, *value*, *color*, and *space*. The aforementioned wire sculpture by Richard Lippold uses lines while the assemblages of Louise Nevelson consist of found objects (shapes, or areas) combined and arranged into a three-dimensional piece. *The Thinker* by Auguste Rodin has a textural quality through the expressive marks Rodin made with his fingers. All three-dimensional art incorporates value because there will always be light wrapping around the sculpture, creating highlights and shadows. Duane Hansen's *Tourists* shows realistic human figures with a representative use of color while Alexander Calder's *Red Gongs* mobile uses primary colors in a decorative approach. Three-dimensional pieces use the design element of space because they contain and possess actual space or the illusion of space. For example, Claes Oldenberg's *Clothespin* has actual dimension whereas the bronze panels in Ghiberti's *The Gates of Paradise* use incised lines and bas-relief figures to create the illusion of space.

Materials

- watercolor paints
- 8-by-11-inch handout with the following design:

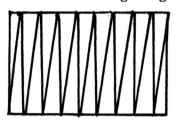

The markings should be 1 inch apart.

- plastic straws
- watercolor paints
- polymer gloss medium
- paintbrush
- plastic meat trays or wax paper
- thread, string, yarn, or ribbon for stringing beads
- scissors

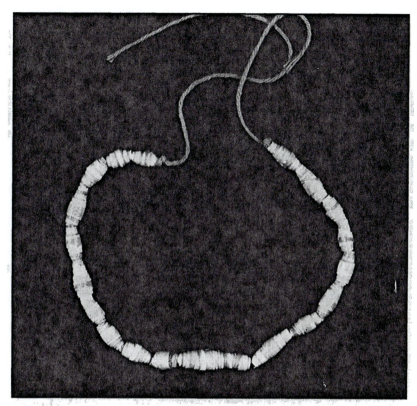

Directions

Have students:

1. Using watercolor paints, paint washes of analogous colors across the handout. Let dry.

2. Cut out along the lines.

3. Roll one triangular shape onto straw starting with the wide end.

4. Brush a polymer gloss medium on the rolled paper to create beads. Remove the beads immediately from the straw and place on plastic tray or wax paper so the bead does not stick. Let dry (have students write their names on the meat tray or wax paper).

5. Thread the beads onto string, yarn, thread, or ribbon. (Option: The paper beads may be combined with clay beads.)

Design Element: Three-dimensional—manipulation, addition; Color—color theory

Art History: Egyptian, Native American, and other primitive cultures who used beads

Grade Level: Lower primary and up

Brain Pot

Materials

- Vaseline
- plastic margarine tub
- clay or Sculpey
- glaze
- kiln

Directions

Have students:

1. With Vaseline, coat the inside surface of a plastic margarine tub.

2. Make clay coils, balls, or other shapes and place one layer on the bottom and the inside wall of the plastic margarine tub.

3. Gently smooth together the clay shapes (pressing too hard will flatten the coils against the surface of the tub; however, the inside surface of the clay should appear smooth—this will ensure that the clay pot stays in one piece once removed from the tub)

4. Carefully remove the clay pot from the tub (note: If this activity cannot be completed in one class period, place a damp paper towel on the clay and place inside a plastic bag so that it will stay moist until firing).

5. Bisque fire, glaze, and glaze fire or with Sculpey, follow directions for baking.

Design Element: Three-dimensional—addition

Art History: Louise Nevelson for addition

Grade Level: Intermediate

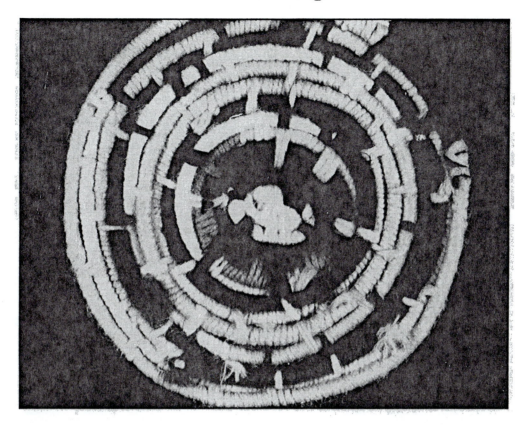

Materials

- six yards of ¼-inch diameter coiling core
- yarn (variety of colors)
- plastic tapestry needles
- scissors

Directions

Have students:

1. Choose three colors of yarn.

2. (Note: At lower grade levels, the teacher should perform this step.) Tie on yarn two inches from the end of the coiling core. Wrap yarn around the core to the end of core. Roll the core into a circle. Using yarn, wrap the yarn and stitch through the center of the rolled core so that it holds its shape.

3. Wrap the yarn 10 times around the core, then stitch three times around two rows of the core. Continue to wrap 10 times and stitch three times.

4. Change colors of yarn at any time by cutting and tying on a new piece.

5. To finish, stitch around two rows of core three times, then slip the yarn under the stitches to hide the end of the yarn.

Design Element: Three-dimensional—addition

Art History: Native American basket weaving using coiling core for addition

Grade Level: Intermediate

Pop-Up Repetition

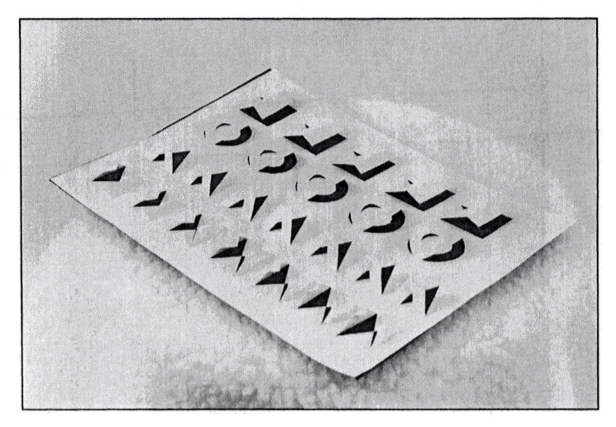

Materials

- two sheets of 12-by-18-inch construction paper
- glue
- X-ACTO knife*
- pencil

Directions

Have students:

1. With pencil, plan a repeating design using at least three of the following shapes:

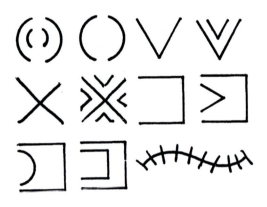

---

*Review with students safety precautions in using knives. Cut away from your hand. Do not walk around with the knife. Have cardboard underneath. Do not talk while cutting. Knives are not toys.

2. Draw the pattern on 12-by-18-inch construction paper. This will be the backside of the finished project.

3. Cut the lines with an X-ACTO knife.

4. Fold up the shapes created by the cutting of designs.

5. Glue a second piece of construction paper to the back side (where designs were originally planned on the first piece of construction paper).

Design Element: Three-dimensional—manipulation; Composition—repetition

Art History: Yaacov Agam for manipulation

Grade Level: Intermediate

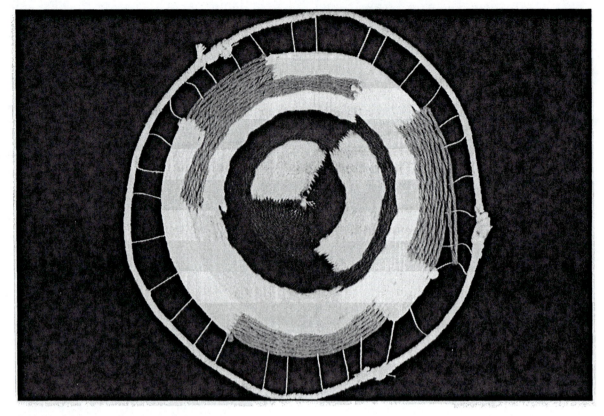

Materials

- 12-inch-diameter cardboard circle template
- 12-by-18-inch posterboard
- scissors
- warp yarn
- weaving yarn
- coat hanger
- pencil

Directions

Have students:

1. Trace the circle template onto posterboard. Cut out the circle.

2. Mark off every inch around the circumference of the circle.

3. Cut ½ inch in (toward the center of the circle) at each mark.

4. For the warp, the threads that will be woven through, start at any slot with warp yarn: place the yarn into the starting slot, across the front of the circle into the slot directly opposite, into an immediately neighboring slot, and back across the circle to the slot directly opposite (the yarn should end at a slot that neighbors the starting slot, forming an *X*). Repeat until all slots have been used.

5. Cut the yarn and tie the ends together.

6. Choose three colors of weaving yarn. Tie one color of yarn onto any warp yarn and push it down to the center. Weave on the outside and then push towards the center. Go over and under each warp yarn to create five rows, weaving with the weft threads, the yarn that is woven through warp yarn. Each row should be opposite of the previous one (if the weft yarn goes over the warp yarn the first time, the next time it goes under). Tie on a different color yarn at any time.

7. Continue weaving until one inch from the edge of the circle is left.

8. Bend a coat hanger into a circle and weave it completely around the warp yarn on the outside of the circle. Twist together the ends of the coat hanger to remove the posterboard, gently bend the notched edges of posterboard up or down so the warp yarn slips off the posterboard.

9. Wrap yarn around the coat hanger. Once the notched posterboard has been removed, the warp threads will be in a V shape at the coat hanger—not ½ inch apart. Be sure to wrap around the original warp yarns to pull the weaving tight again by wrapping the yarn around the coat hanger so the warp threads are once again separated by ½ inch.

Design Element: Three-dimensional—fiber art, warp and weft

Art History: Navajo and other Native American weaving for addition

Grade Level: Upper elementary

Materials

- 9-by-12-inch paper
- 12-by-16½-inch tagboard
- X-ACTO knife*
- ruler
- pencil

Directions

Have students:

Note: Steps 1–6 are for practice.

1. On 9-by-12-inch paper, use a ruler and pencil to draw a 4-by-8-inch box with the long side vertical.

2. Inside the box, mark one inch from the top and the bottom of the box and ½ inch from the two sides of the box to create a 3-by-6-inch box inside the 4-by-8-inch box. Draw a vertical line down the center of the box from top to bottom.

3. Mark off every ½ inch to make horizontal lines inside the 3-by-6-inch box (see figure).

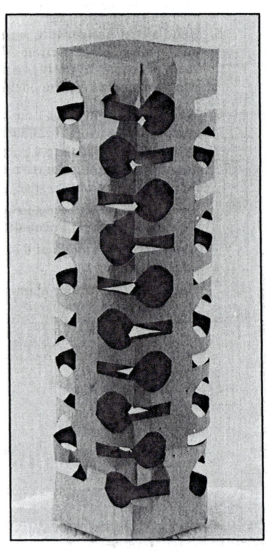

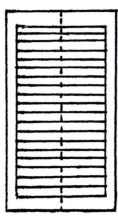

4. Create a repeating line design. The repeating lines must be ½ inch apart. Possible repeating line designs are:

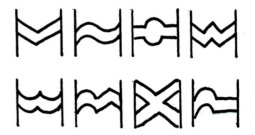

5. Cut along repeating lines. Do not cut the vertical lines of the 3-by-6-inch box. Nothing should be cut out. Cut only the horizontal repeating lines.

6. Fold paper in half along vertical center line. Open paper, push in alternating strips and crease at the end of the cuts to reverse the fold.

*Review with students safety precautions in using knives. Cut away from your hand. Do not walk around with the knife. Have cardboard underneath. Do not talk while cutting. Knives are not toys.

7. For the final project: On 12-by-16½-inch paper, mark off every 4 inches at the top and bottom of the 16½-inch edges. You should have ½ inch left over. This will be your flap to glue the rectangular prism together.

8. Draw original design in each 4-inch wide space. You will draw the design from step 5 four times.

9. Cut the horizontal line design.

10. Fold at the center vertical line in each of the four sections. Glue at the ½-inch flap to create a rectangular prism.

11. Push in alternating strips as in step 6.

Design Element: Three-dimensional—manipulation; Composition—repetition

Art History: Agam for manipulation

Grade Level: Upper elementary

Pop-Up Name

Materials

- ruler
- 12-by-18-inch tagboard
- X-ACTO knife*
- 12-by-18-inch construction paper
- pencil
- glue

Directions

Have students:

1. Fold a sheet of 12-by-18-inch tagboard paper in half lengthwise.
2. Mark off two inches on each side of the fold to create two parallel guidelines.
3. Find the center of the fold and have students determine the center letter or space of their name.
4. Have students write their names backwards with reversed letters between the guidelines.
5. Score the tops of the letters where they touch the guidelines. To score, open up a pair of scissors, position a ruler on the guide line, and gently press the point of the scissors along the edge of the ruler to create a crease.
6. Use an X-ACTO knife to cut the lines of the letters. Do not cut a letter where it touches the guide line (i.e., do not cut out the letter).
7. Fold the paper in, and fold the letters out by reversing the fold at the ends of the cuts.
8. For a backing, glue a colored piece of 12-by-18-inch construction paper on back of the tagboard by putting glue on the paper with the letters.

Design Element: Three-dimensional—manipulation

Art History: Agam for manipulation

Grade Level: Upper elementary

*Review with students safety precautions in using knives. Cut away from your hand. Do not walk around with the knife. Have cardboard underneath. Do not talk while cutting. Knives are not toys.

Materials

- 9-by-12-inch drawing paper
- portrait guideline
- clay rolled into 9-by-12-inch slab, ¼-inch thick
- kiln
- mirror
- scissors
- pencil
- paintbrush
- glazes or tempera paint
- polymer medium or varnish

Directions

Have students:

1. Using pencil and drawing paper, draw a self-portrait—in proportion and in a real-life scale—while looking in a mirror.

2. Cut away the background and lay the portrait drawing on a slab of clay.

3. Transfer the drawing to clay by poking small holes along the lines with a very sharp pencil.

4. Remove the paper and connect the dots with a blunt pencil point.

5. Bisque fire.

6. Glaze and glaze fire or paint with tempera paint and coat with polymer medium or varnish.

Design Element: Three-dimensional—bas relief, three dimensional art with shallow projections from a surface

Art History: Lorenzo Ghiberti for bas relief

Grade Level: Upper elementary

Glossary

achromatic: the lack of color; the use of black, grays, and white.

addition: the assembling of material or materials to create three-dimensional art.

ambiguous space: the placement of objects in a setting where they cannot exist together in reality or the objects' proportion and scale are distorted.

analogous colors: adjacent colors on the color wheel.

approximate symmetry: the arrangement of similar objects on both sides of an imagined center line in a composition.

area: the two-dimensional silhouette shape of an object.

art concepts: the design elements and/or principles of organization.

art history: the chronicle of artistic periods and styles.

asymmetrical balance: the random placement of objects in a composition that counter balance each other.

atmospheric perspective: the illusion of depth created as colors are toned down, or neutralized, on receding objects in a composition.

balance: the placement of objects on a picture plane so that every part of the picture plane becomes an integral part of the composition.

bas-relief: three-dimensional art with slightly raised areas on the surface.

biomorphic shapes: shapes drawn with curved lines.

calligraphic line: a line that varies in width.

character: the use of design elements to portray human characteristics (e.g., a silly line).

chiaroscuro: pictorial representation showing objects with values; to show highlights and shadows.

collage: a piece of art made by attaching any material or item to a surface.

color: the sensation resulting from stimulation of the retina of the eye by light waves; the study of the color wheel.

color wheel: the circular arrangement of colors from a prism; red, orange, yellow, green, blue, then violet.

complementary colors: colors opposite each other on the color wheel; yellow and violet, blue and orange, red and green.

composition: also called form, the arrangement of objects on a picture plane.

converging parallels: two lines that meet at a point on or off the picture plane to create the illusion of space.

cool colors: colors that appear to recede from the viewer; blues, greens, and violets.

decoration: use of the design elements to adorn or enrich a composition with two-dimensional patterns of lines, shapes, values, colors, and textures.

descriptive texture: a pictorial representation of how an object feels through careful study and rendering of the lines and shapes that make up the surfaces of an object; also called simulated texture and objective texture.

dominance: an object or objects used as a focal point(s), an object or objects that appear dominant in a composition.

economy: the process of balancing a composition so that it does not contain too many shapes, values, textures, or colors.

emotion: the use of design elements to portray emotion (e.g., use of blue, green, and violet to portray sadness).

encaustic texture: the surface of a piece of art that has actual texture.

felt composition: the arrangement of objects on a picture plane to afford a sense of balance and equilibrium.

focal point: object or objects that appear to be the center of interest in a composition.

form: also called composition, the arrangement of objects on a picture plane.

fractional space: portraying more than one view of an object in one composition.

geometric perspective: a method of drawing to create the illusion of space through lines converging at a vanishing point.

geometric shapes: objects drawn with straight lines.

hard edges: lines created in a composition when one color, value, or texture ends and another color, value, or texture begins.

harmony: objects appear to compliment each other or appear similar in a composition.

high contrast: the use of black, white, and few grays in a composition.

highlight: in achromatic value, the lightest area on the surface of an object.

horizon line: in geometric perspective, the line that represents where the sky meets the earth.

hue: a specific color.

intensity: the purity of a color.

interpenetration: creating the illusion of space by drawing objects that appear to penetrate or go through each other.

invented texture: textures used to decorate a picture plane; not necessarily descriptive.

kinesthetic sight: referring to the human eye's ability to focus on one object at a time.

light: in value, the lightest gray on an achromatic surface.

line: a long, thin mark made with any media on a surface.

local colors: the actual colors that make up the surface of an object.

low contrast: with value, to use mostly grays and little black and white.

manipulation: in three-dimensional art, the reshaping or rearrangement of a medium.

meaning: (see purpose)

media: the materials used to create a piece of art.

message: the visual representation of feelings and thoughts that an artist relays through a piece of art.

monochromatic colors: a color scheme with tints, tones, and shades of one color.

motif: an object or pattern that repeats in a composition.

movement: how the viewer's eye moves around a composition.

multiple light: in value, light that covers an object from all angles; tends to visually flatten an object because the values become uniform.

negative shapes: the background shapes in a composition; shapes in between and around objects.

non-objective approach: a composition that contains no recognizable objects.

non-representative: (see non-objective approach)

objective approach: the realistic depiction of the subject matter.

objective texture: (see descriptive texture)

one-point perspective: a drawing system to create the illusion of space; all receding lines converge at one vanishing point on a horizon line.

overlap: to create the illusion of space on a picture plane by drawing two overlapping opaque objects.

papier-collé: a form of collage incorporating torn or cut paper to decorate a picture plane.

penumbra: in value, the medium gray areas on an achromatic surface.

picture plane: the actual surface area of a composition.

plastic quality: the study of a design element, media, or technique; communication is not a concern.

position: in space, the placement of an object lower in the picture plane to create the illusion that it is closer to the viewer.

positive shapes: the two-dimensional shape of an object; the silhouette shape of an object.

primary colors: red, yellow and blue; colors that cannot be made by mixing any other two colors.

principles of organization: in a composition, the concerns of design and balance that make a composition visually appealing; the necessary considerations for a balanced composition.

proportion: objects and shapes that are drawn in scale to each other in terms of size and number.

purpose: the reason for the creation of a piece of art; the study of an art concept, the exploration of the plastic quality of a media or design element, or as a means of communication.

radial composition: a composition that repeats in a circular fashion around a center point.

repetitive composition: a composition containing some type of repeating pattern, whether very simple or complex.

secondary colors: colors created by the mixture of two primary colors; green, violet, orange.

shade: to add black to a color.

simulated texture: (see descriptive texture)

simultaneous contrast: an optical illusion; the viewer senses a different color than the actual color present because of the effect of an adjacent, contrasting color.

size: in space, the larger objects on a picture plane appear closer to the viewer.

soft edges: the subtle transition between shapes of colors, values, or textures.

space: the use of lines, shapes, values, colors, and textures to create the illusion of depth on a two-dimensional surface.

stereoscopic sight: perception of space; the human brain combines two slightly different views which creates depth perception.

subject matter: the object(s) chosen for a composition; drawn either objectively, subjectively, or non-objectively.

subjective approach: personal interpretation of the subject matter; may be simplified or abstracted but the object remains recognizable.

substitution: in three-dimensional art, the use of a mold to create a piece of art.

subtraction: in three-dimensional art, the process of carving to remove material to create a piece of art.

symmetrical composition: an object has a mirror image on the opposite side of an imagined center line.

technique: how the media or medium is used to create a piece of art.

tenebrism: in value, the representation of figures partially hidden in shadow.

tertiary colors: colors created by mixing adjacent colors on the color wheel.

texture: the representation of the "feel" of an object's surface.

tint: to add white to a color.

tone: to mix two complementary colors; colors become toned-down or neutralized.

triadic colors: colors that form an equilateral triangle on the color wheel.

umbra: in value, the darkest area on an achromatic surface.

unity: every component of a composition contributes to a visually appealing and/or expressive piece of art.

vanishing point: in geometric perspective, the dot placed on the horizon line at which receding lines converge.

variety: a contrast or a variation of objects within a composition that provides interest and/or uniqueness.

warm colors: colors that appear to be visually closer to the viewer; red, orange, yellow.

Index

About the Author

Del Klaustermeier, an art educator since 1972, has taught art at the elementary, secondary, and college levels. With a Bachelor of Art in Art Education from Concordia University, River Forest, Illinois, and a Master of Arts from the University of Northern Colorado, Greeley, Del presently is an assistant professor at Concordia University, River Forest, Illinois. Del previously taught in the Lutheran high school systems in Chicago, Illinois and Denver, Colorado; Jefferson County Public Schools, Golden, Colorado; The Art Students League of Denver, Colorado; and served as adjunct faculty for Chapman University's Denver Center, The University of Northern Colorado's College of Continuing Education, and Lesley College's National Outreach program. He has led numerous in-services and workshops and has taken part in various art exhibits and competitions.

from *Teacher Ideas Press*

GLUES, BREWS, AND GOOS
Recipes and Formulas for Almost Any Classroom Project
Diana F. Marks

You've got to have it! This indispensable activity book pulls together hundreds of practical, easy recipes and formulas for classroom projects. From paints and salt map mixtures to volcanic action formulas, these kid-tested projects make learning authentic and enjoyable. All projects use ingredients that are easy to find and processes that are up-to-date. **Grades K–6.**
xvi, 179p. 8½x11 paper ISBN 1-56308-362-0

SCIENCE THROUGH CHILDREN'S LITERATURE, 2d Edition
Carol M. Butzow and John W. Butzow

The Butzows' groundbreaking, critically acclaimed, and best-selling resource has been thoroughly revised and updated with new titles and new activities for today's classroom. More than 30 exciting instructional units integrate all areas of the curriculum and serve as models to educators at all levels. Adopted as a supplementary text in schools of education nationwide, this resource features outstanding children's fiction books that are rich in scientific concepts yet equally well known for their strong story lines and universal appeal. **Grades K–3.**
xix, 205p. 8½x11 paper ISBN 1-56308-651-4

MULTICULTURAL FOLKTALES
Readers Theatre for Elementary Students
Suzanne I. Barchers

Introduce your students to other countries and cultures through these engaging readers theatre scripts based upon traditional folk and fairy tales. Representing more than 30 countries and regions, the 40 reproducible scripts are accompanied by presentation suggestions and recommendations for props and delivery. **Grades 1–5.**
xxi, 188p. 8½x11 paper ISBN 1-56308-760-X

SUPER SIMPLE STORYTELLING
A Can-Do Guide for Every Classroom, Every Day
Kendall Haven

Aside from guides to more than 40 powerful storytelling exercises, you'll find the Golden List of what an audience really needs from storytelling, a proven, step-by-step system for successfully learning and remembering a story, and the Great-Amazing-Never-Fail Safety Net to prevent storytelling disasters. This system has been successfully used by more than 15,000 educators across the country. **All Levels.**
xxvii, 229p. 8½x11 paper ISBN 1-56308-681-6

MORE SOCIAL STUDIES THROUGH CHILDREN'S LITERATURE
An Integrated Approach
Anthony D. Fredericks

These dynamic literature-based activities will help you energize the social studies curriculum and implement national and state standards. Each of these 33 units offers book summaries, social studies topic areas, critical thinking questions, and dozens of easy-to-do activities for every grade level. The author also gives practical guidelines for integrating literature across the curriculum, lists of Web sites useful in social studies classes, and annotated bibliographies of related resources. **Grades K–5.**
xix, 225p. 8½x11 paper ISBN 1-56308-761-8

For a free catalog or to place an order, please contact:
Teacher Ideas Press • Dept. B050 • P.O. Box 6633 • Englewood, CO • 80155-6633
800-237-6124 • www.lu.com/tip • Fax: 303-220-8843